Matthew Arnold

Civilization in the United States

First and last Impressions of America

Matthew Arnold

Civilization in the United States
First and last Impressions of America

ISBN/EAN: 9783337110819

Printed in Europe, USA, Canada, Australia, Japan

Cover: Foto ©ninafisch / pixelio.de

More available books at **www.hansebooks.com**

CIVILIZATION
IN THE UNITED STATES

FIRST AND LAST IMPRESSIONS
OF AMERICA

BY

MATTHEW ARNOLD

———

BOSTON
CUPPLES AND HURD
PUBLISHERS
1888

THIRD EDITION.

CONTENTS.

GENERAL GRANT.

GENERAL GRANT.

PART I.

I HAVE heard it said, I know not with what
degree of truth, that while the sale in America
of General Grant's *Personal Memoirs* has produced three hundred thousand dollars for the
benefit of his widow and family, there have not
in England been sold of the book three hundred
copies.   Certainly the book has had no wide
circulation here, it has not been much read or
much discussed.   There are obvious reasons for
this.   The book relates in great detail the military history of the American Civil War, so far
as Grant bore part in it ; such a history cannot
possibly have for other nations the interest
which it has for the United States themselves.
For the general reader outside of America, it
certainly cannot ; as to the value and importance
of the history to the military specialist, that is
a question on which I hear very conflicting opinions expressed, and one on which I myself can

have, of course, no opinion to offer. So far as
the general European reader might still be attracted to such a history, in spite of its military
details, for the sake of the importance of the
issues at stake and of the personages engaged, we
in Europe have, it cannot be denied, in approaching an American recital of the deeds of "the
greatest nation upon earth," some apprehension
and mistrust to get over. We may be pardoned
for doubting whether we shall in the recital find
measure, whether we shall find sobriety. Then,
too, General Grant, the central figure of these
Memoirs, is not to the English imagination the
hero of the American Civil War ; the hero is
Lee, and of Lee the *Memoirs* tell us little.
Moreover General Grant, when he was in England, did not himself personally interest people
much. Later he fell in America into the hands
of financing speculators, and his embarrass-
ments, though they excited sorrow and compas-
sion, did not at all present themselves to us as
those of "a good man struggling with adversity."
For all these reasons, then, the *Personal Memoirs*
have in England been received with coldness and
indifference.

I, too, had seen General Grant in England, and
did not find him interesting. If I said the truth,
I should say that I thought him ordinary-looking,

dull and silent. An expression of gentleness and even sweetness in the eyes, which the portraits in the *Memoirs* show, escaped me. A strong, resolute, business-like man, who by possession of unlimited resources in men and money, and by the unsparing use of them, had been enabled to wear down and exhaust the strength of the South, this was what I supposed Grant to be, this and little more.

Some documents published by General Badeau in the American newspapers first attracted my serious attention to Grant. Among those documents was a letter from him which showed qualities for which, in the rapid and uncharitable view which our cursory judgments of men so often take, I had by no means given him credit. It was the letter of a man with the virtue, rare everywhere, but more rare in America, perhaps, than anywhere else, the virtue of being able to confront and resist popular clamour, the *civium ardor prava jubentium*. Public opinion seemed in favour of a hard and insolent course, the authorities seemed putting pressure upon Grant to make him follow it. He resisted with firmness and dignity. After reading that letter I turned to General Grant's *Personal Memoirs*, then just published. This man, I said to myself, deserves respect and attention ; and I read the two bulky volumes through.

I found shown in them a man, strong, resolute, and business-like, as Grant had appeared to me when I first saw him ; a man with no magical personality, touched by no divine light and giving out none.　I found a language all astray in its use of *will* and *shall, should* and *would,* an English employing the verb *to conscript* and the participle *conscripting,* and speaking in a despatch to the Secretary of War of having *badly whipped* the enemy ; an English without charm and without high breeding.　But at the same time I found a man of sterling good-sense as well as of the firmest resolution ; a man, withal, humane, simple, modest ; from all restless self-consciousness and desire for display perfectly free ; never boastful where he himself was concerned, and where his nation was concerned seldom boastful, boastful only in circumstances where nothing but high genius or high training, I suppose, can save an American from being boastful. I found a language straightforward, nervous, firm, possessing in general the high merit of saying clearly in the fewest possible words what had to be said, and saying it, frequently, with shrewd and unexpected turns of expression.　The *Memoirs* renewed and completed the expression which the letter given by General Badeau had made upon me.　And now I want to enable

Grant and his *Memoirs* as far as possible to speak for themselves to the English public, which knows them, I believe, as imperfectly as a few months ago I myself did.

General Grant was born at Point Pleasant, in the State of Ohio, on the 27th of April, 1822. His name, *Ulysses,* makes one think of *Tristram Shandy;* but how often do American names make one think of *Tristram Shandy!* The father of the little Ulysses followed the trade of a tanner; he was a constant reader both of books and newspapers, and "before he was twenty years of age was a constant contributor," his son tells us, "to Western newspapers, and was also, from that time, until he was fifty years old, an able debater in the societies for this purpose, which were then common in the West." Of many and many an American farmer and tradesman this is the history. General Grant, however, never shared the paternal and national love for public speaking. As to his schooling, he never, he tells us, missed a quarter from school, from the time he was old enough to attend till the time when he left home, at the age of seventeen, for the Military Academy at West Point. But the instruction in the country schools at that time was very poor :—

"A single teacher—who was often a man or a woman incapable of teaching much, even if they imparted all they knew—would have thirty or forty scholars, male and female, from the infant learning the A B C, up to the young lady of eighteen and the boy of twenty studying the highest branches taught—the three R's. I never saw an algebra, or other mathematical work higher than the arithmetic, until after I was appointed to West Point. I then bought a work on algebra in Cincinnati; but, having no teacher, it was Greek to me."

This schooling is unlike that of our young gentlemen preparing for Sandhurst or Woolwich, but still more unlike theirs is Grant's life out of school-hours. He has told us how regularly he attended his school, such as it was. He proceeds:

"This did not exempt me from labour. In my early days, every one laboured more or less in the region where my youth was spent, and more in proportion to their private means. It was only the very poor who were exempt. While my father carried on the manufacture of leather and worked at the trade himself, he owned and tilled considerable land. I detested the trade, preferring almost any other labour; but I was fond of agriculture and of all employments in which horses were used. We had, among other lands, fifty acres of forest within a mile of the village. In the fall of the year choppers were employed to cut enough wood to last a twelve-month. When I was seven or eight years of age I began hauling all the wood used in the house and shops. I could not load it on the wagons, of course, at that time, but I could drive, and the choppers would load, and some one at the house unload. When about eleven years old, I was strong enough to hold a plough. From that age until seventeen I did all the work done with horses, such as breaking up the land, furrowing, ploughing corn and potatoes, bringing in the crops when harvested, hauling all the wood, besides tending two or three horses, a cow or two, and sawing wood for stoves, &c., while still attending school. For this I was compensated by the fact that there never was any scolding or punishing by my parents : no objection to rational enjoyments, such as fishing, going to the creek a mile away to swim in summer ; taking a horse and visiting my grandparents in the adjoining county, fifteen miles off ; skating on the ice in winter, or taking a horse and sleigh when there was snow on the ground."

The bringing up of Abraham Lincoln was also, I suppose, much on this wise ; and meagre, too meagre, as may have been the schooling, I confess I am inclined on the whole to exclaim : "What a wholesome bringing up it was!"

I must find room for one story of Grant's boyhood, a story which he tells against himself :—

"There was a Mr. Ralston living within a few miles of the village, who owned a colt that I very much wanted. My father had offered twenty dollars for it, but Ralston wanted twenty-five. I was so anxious to have the colt, that, after the owner left, I begged to be allowed to take him at the price demanded. My father yielded, but said twenty dollars was all the horse was worth, and told me to offer that price; if it was not accepted, I might offer twenty-two and a half, and if that would not get him, might give the twenty-five. I at once mounted a horse and went for the colt. When I got to Mr. Ralston's house, I said to him : 'Papa says I may offer you twenty dollars for the colt, but if you won't take that, I am to offer twenty-two and a half, and if you won't take that, to give you twenty-five.' It would not require a Connecticut man to guess the price finally agreed upon. I could not have been over eight years old at the time. This transaction caused me great heart-burning. The story got amongst the boys of the village, and it was a long time before I heard the last of it."

The boys of the village may well have been amused. How astounding to find an American boy so little "'cute," so little "smart." But how delightful also, and how refreshing; how full of promise for the boy's future character! Grant came in later life to see straight and to see clear, more than most men, more than even most Americans, whose virtue it is that in matters within their range they see straight and see clear; but he never was in the least "smart," and it is one of his merits.

The United States Senator for Ohio procured for young Grant, when he was seventeen years old, a nomination to West Point. He was not himself eager for it. His father one day said to him : "Ulysses, I believe you are going to receive the appointment." "What appointment?" I enquired. "To West Point; I have applied for it." "But I won't go," I said. He said he thought I would, *and I thought so too, if he did.* I really had no objection to going to West Point, except that I had a very exalted idea of the acquirements necessary to get through. I did not believe I possessed them, and could not bear the idea of failing."

He did go. Although he had no military ardour he desired to see the world. Already he had seen more of it than most of the boys of his

village ; he had visited Cincinnati, the principal
city of his native State, and Louisville, the
principal city of the adjoining State of Kentucky ; he had also been out as far as Wheeling
in Virginia, and now, if he went to West Point,
he would have the opportunity of seeing Philadelphia and New York. "When these places
were visited," he says, "I would have been glad
to have had a steamboat or railroad collision, or
any other accident happen, by which I might
have received a temporary injury sufficient to
make me ineligible for awhile to enter the Academy." He took his time on the road, and having left home in the middle of May, did not
arrive at West Point until the end of the month.
Two weeks later he passed his examination for
admission, very much, he tells us, to his surprise.
But none of his professional studies interested
him, though he did well in mathematics, which
he found, he says, very easy to him. Throughout his first year he found the life tedious, read
novels, and had no intention of remaining in
the army, even if he should succeed in graduating at the end of his four years' course, a
success which he did not expect to attain.
When in 1839 a Bill was discussed in Congress
for abolishing the Military Academy, he hoped
the Bill might pass, and so set him free. But

it did not pass, and a year later he would have been sorry, he says, if it had passed, although he still found his life at West Point dull. His last two years went quicker than his first two; but they still seemed to him "about five times as long as Ohio years." At last all his examinations were passed, he was appointed to an infantry regiment, and, before joining, went home on leave with a desperate cough and a stature which had run up too fast for his strength.

In September, 1843, he joined his regiment, the 4th United States infantry, at Jefferson Barracks, St. Louis. No doubt his training at West Point, an establishment with a public and high standing, and with serious studies, had been invaluable to him. But still he had no desire to remain in the army. At St. Louis he met and became attached to a young lady whom he afterwards married, Miss Dent, and his hope was to become an assistant professor of mathematics at West Point. With this hope he re-read at Jefferson Barracks his West Point mathematics, and pursued a course of historical study also. But the Mexican war came on and kept him in the army.

With the annexation of Texas in prospect, Grant's regiment was moved to Fort Jessup, on

the western border of Louisiana. Ostensibly
the American troops were to prevent filibuster-
ing into Texas; really they were sent as a
menace to Mexico in case she appeared to con-
template war. Grant's life in Louisiana was
pleasant. He had plenty of professional duty,
many of his brother officers having been de-
tailed on special duty away from the regiment.
He gave up the thought of becoming a teacher
of mathematics, and read only for his own
amusement, "and not very much for that;" he
kept a horse and rode, visited the planters on
the Red River; and was out of doors the whole
day nearly; and so he quite recovered from the
cough, and the threatenings of consumption,
which he had carried with him from West
Point. "I have often thought," he adds, "that
my life was saved, and my health restored, by
exercise and exposure enforced by an administrative act and a war, both of which I dis-
approved."

For disapprove the menace to Mexico, and
the subsequent war, he did. One lingers over
a distinguished man's days of growth and for-
mation, so important for all which is to come
after. And already, under young Grant's plain
exterior and air of indifference, there had grown
up in him an independent and sound judgment.

"Generally the officers of the army were indif-
ferent whether the annexation was consum-
mated or not; but not so all of them. For myself, I was bitterly opposed to the measure, and
to this day regard the war which resulted as one
of the most unjust ever waged by a stronger
against a weaker nation."

Texas was annexed, a territory larger than
the Austrian Empire; and after taking military
possession of Texas, the American army of
occupation, under General Taylor, went on and
occupied some more disputed territory beyond.
Even here they did not stop, but went further
on still, meaning apparently to force the Mexicans to attack them and begin war. "We were
sent to provoke war, but it was essential that
Mexico should commence it. It was very doubtful whether Congress would declare war; but if
Mexico should attack our troops, the Executive
could announce: 'Whereas war exists by the
acts of, etc.,' and prosecute the contest with
vigour. Once initiated, there were few public
men who would have the courage to oppose it."

Incensed at the Americans fortifying themselves on the Rio Grande, opposite Matamoras,
the Mexicans at last fired the necessary shot,
and the war was commenced. This was in
March 1846. In September 1847 the American

army entered the city of Mexico. Vera Cruz, Puebla, and other principal cities of the country, were already in their possession. In February 1848 was signed the treaty which gave to the United States Texas with the Rio Grande for its boundary, and the whole territory then included in New Mexico and Upper California. For New Mexico and California, however, the Americans paid a sum of fifteen millions of dollars.

Grant marks with sagacity and justness the causes and effects of the Mexican war. As the North grew in numbers and population, the South required more territory to counterbalance it; to maintain through this wide territory the institution of slavery, it required to have control of the national Government. With great energy and ability, it obtained this control; it acquired Texas and other large regions for slavery; it proceeded to use the powers of Government, in the North as well as in the South, for the purpose of securing and maintaining its hold upon its slaves. But the wider the territory over which slavery was spread, and the more numerous the slaves, the greater became the difficulty of making this hold quite secure, and the stronger grew the irritation of the North to see the powers and laws of the whole nation used for the purpose. The Fugitive Slave Law brought this irritation to its height, made it uncontrollable, and the War of Secession was the result. "The Southern rebellion," says Grant, "was largely the outgrowth of the Mexican war. Nations, like individuals, are punished for their transgressions. We got our punishment in the most sanguinary and expensive war of modern times."

The part of Grant in the Mexican war was of course that of a young subaltern only, and is described by him with characteristic modesty. He showed, however, of what good stuff he was made, and his performances with a certain howitzer in a church-steeple so pleased his general that he sent for Grant, commended him, and ordered a second howitzer to be placed at his disposal. A captain of voltigeurs came with the gun in charge. "I could not tell the general," says Grant, "that there was not room enough in the steeple for another gun, because he probably would have looked upon such a statement as a contradiction from a second lieutenant. I took the captain with me, but did not use his gun."

When the evacuation of Mexico was completed, Grant married, in August 1848, Miss Julia Dent, to whom he had been engaged more

than four years. For two years the young cou-
ple lived at Detroit in Michigan, where Grant
was now stationed ; he was then ordered to the
Pacific coast. It was settled that Mrs. Grant
should, during his absence, live with her own
family in St. Louis. The regiment went first
to Aspinwall, then to California and Oregon.
In 1853 Grant became captain, but he had now
two children, and saw no chance of supporting
his family on his pay as an army officer. He
determined to resign, and in the following year
he did so. He left the Pacific coast, he tells
us, very much attached to it, and with the full
intention of one day making his home there, an
intention which he did not abandon until, in the
winter of 1863–4, Congress passed the Act ap-
pointing him Lieutenant-General of the armies
of the United States.

His life on leaving the army offers, like his
early training, a curious contrast to what usually
takes place amongst ourselves. First he tried
farming, on a farm belonging to his wife near
St. Louis ; but he could not make it answer,
though he worked hard. He had insufficient
capital, and more than sufficient fever and ague.
After four years he established a partnership
with a cousin of his wife named Harry Boggs,
in a real estate agency business in St. Louis. He

found that the business was not more than one person could do, and not enough to support two families. So he withdrew from the co-partnership with Boggs, and in ·May 1860 removed to Galena, Illinois, and took a clerkship in a leather shop there belonging to his father.

Politics now began to interest him, and his reflexions on them at the moment when the War of Secession was approaching I must quote :

" Up to the Mexican war there were a few out and out abolitionists, men who carried their hostility to slavery into all elections, from those for a justice of the peace up to the Presidency of the United States. They were noisy but not numerous. But the great majority of people at the North, where slavery did not exist, were opposed to the institution, and looked upon its existence in any part of the country as unfortunate. They did not hold the States where slavery existed responsible for it, and believed that protection should be given to the right of property in slaves until some satisfactory way could be reached to be rid of the institution. Opposition to slavery was a creed of neither political party. But with the inauguration of the Mexican war, in fact with the annexation of Texas, the inevitable conflict commenced. As

the time for the Presidental election of 1856 —
the first at which I had the opportunity of voting
— approached, party feeling began to run high."

Grant himself voted in 1856 for Buchanan,
the candidate of the Slave States, because he
saw clearly, he says, that in the exasperation of
feeling at that time, the election of a Republican
President meant the secession of all the Slave
States, and the plunging of the country into a
war of which no man could foretell the issue.
He hoped that in the course of the next four
years — the Slave States having got a President
of their own choice, and being without a pretext
for secession — men's passions would quiet
down, and the catastrophe be averted.   Even if
it was not, he thought the country would by
that time be better prepared to receive the
shock and to resist it.

I am not concerned to discuss Grant's reasons
for his vote, but I wish to remark how com-
pletely his reflexions dispose of the reproaches
addressed so often by Americans to England
for not sympathising with the North attacking
slavery, in a war with the South upholding it.
From what he says it is evident how very far
the North was, when the war began, from attacking slavery.   Grant himself was not for
attacking it; Lincoln was not.   They, and the

North in general, wished "that protection should be given to the right of property in slaves, until some satisfactory way could be reached to be rid of the institution." England took the North at its word, and regarded its struggle as one for preserving the Union, and the force and greatness which accrue from the Union, not for abolishing slavery. True, far-sighted people here might perceive that the war must probably issue, if the North prevailed, in the abolition of slavery, and might wish well to the North on that account. They did so; coldly, it is true, for the attitude of the North was not such as to call forth enthusiasm, but sincerely. A great number of people in England, on the other hand, looking at the surface of things merely, clearly seeing that the North was not meaning to attack slavery but to uphold the power and grandeur of the United States, thought themselves quite free to wish well to the South, the weaker side which was making a gallant fight, and to favour the breaking up of the Union.

Here was the real offence. The Americans of the North, admiring and valuing their great Republic above all things, could not forgive disfavour or coldness to it; could only impute them to envy and jealousy. Far-sighted people in England might perceive that the main-

tenance of the Union was not only likely to
bring about the emancipation of the slave, but
was also on other grounds to be desired for the
good of the world. Our artisans might be in
sympathy with the popular and unaristocratic
institutions of the United States, and be therefore averse to any weakening of the great Republic. And these feelings prevailed here, as
is well known, so as to govern the course taken
by this country during the War of Secession.
Still, there was much disfavour and more coldness. Americans were, and are, indignant that
the upholding of their great Republic should
have had in England such cold friends, and so
many actual enemies. It is like the indignant
astonishment of George Sand during the German war, "to see Europe looking on with indifference to the danger of such a civilization as
that of France." But admiration and favour
are uncompellable; we admire and favour only
an object which delights us, helps us, elevates
us, and does us good. The thing is to make us
feel that the object does this. Self-admiration
and self-laudation will not convince us; on the
contrary, they indispose us. France would be
more attractive to us if she were less prone to
call herself the head of civilization and the pride
of the world; the United States, if they were

more backward in proclaiming themselves "the greatest nation upon earth."

In 1860 Lincoln was elected President, and the catastrophe, which Grant hoped might have been averted, arrived. He had in 1860 no vote, but things were now come to that pass that he felt compelled to make his choice between minority rule and rule by the majority, and he was glad, therefore, to see Lincoln elected. Secession was imminent, and with secession, war; but Grant confesses that his own views at that time were those officially expressed later on by Mr. Seward, that "the war would be over in ninety days." He retained these views, he tells us, until after the battle of Shiloh.

Lincoln was not to come into office until the spring of 1861. The South was confident and defiant, and in the North there were prominent men and newspapers declaring that the government had no legal right to coerce the South. It was unsafe for Mr. Lincoln, when he went to be sworn into office in March 1861, to travel as President-elect; he had to be smuggled into Washington. When he took on the 4th of March his oath of office to maintain the Union, eleven States had gone out of it. On the 11th of April, Fort Sumter in Charleston harbour was fired upon, and a few days after was captured. Then the President issued a call for 75,000 men. "There was not a State in the North of a million inhabitants," says Grant, "that would not have furnished the entire number faster than arms could have been supplied to them, if it had been necessary."

As soon as news of the call for volunteers reached Galena, where Grant lived, the citizens were summoned to meet at the Court House in the evening. The Court House was crammed. Grant, though a comparative stranger, was called upon to preside, because he had been in the army, and had seen service. "With much embarrassment and some prompting, I made out to announce the object of the meeting." Speeches followed ; then volunteers were called for to form the company which Galena had to furnish. The company was raised, and the officers and non-commissioned officers were elected, before the meeting adjourned. Grant declined the captaincy before the balloting, but promised to help them all he could, and to be found in the service, in some position, if there should actually be war. "I never," he adds, "went into our leather store after that meeting, to put up a package or do other business."

After seeing the company mustered at Springfield, the capital of Illinois, Grant was asked by the Governor of the State to give some help in the military office, where his old army experience enabled him to be of great use. But on the 24th of May he wrote to the Adjutant-General of the Army, saying that, "having been fifteen years in the regular army, including four at West Point, and feeling it the duty of every one who has been educated at the Government expense to offer their services for the support of the Government," he wished to tender his services until the close of the war, "in such capacity as may be offered." He got no answer. He then thought of getting appointed on the staff of General McClellan, whom he had known at West Point, and went to seek the General at Cincinnati. He called twice, but failed to see him. While he was at Cincinnati, however, the President issued his second call for troops, this time for 300,000 men; and the Governor of Illinois, mindful of Grant's recent help, appointed him colonel of the 21st Illinois regiment of infantry. In a month he had brought his regiment into a good state of drill and discipline, and was then ordered to a point on a railroad in Missouri, where an Illinois regiment was surrounded by "rebels." His own account of his first experience as a Commander is very characteristic of him:

"My sensations as we approached what I supposed might be a 'field of battle,' were anything
but agreeable. I had been in all the engage-
ments in Mexico that it was possible for one
person to be in ; but not in command. If some
one else had been colonel, and I had been lieu-
tenant-colonel, I do not think I would have felt
any trepidation. Before we were prepared to
cross the Mississippi River at Quincy, my anxiety was relieved ; for the men of the besieged
regiment came straggling into the town. I am
inclined to think both sides got frightened and
ran away."

Now, however, he was started ; and from this
time until he received Lee's surrender at Appomattox Court House, four years later, he was
always the same strong man, showing the same
valuable qualities. He had not the pathos and
dignity of Lee, his power of captivating the
admiring interest, almost the admiring affection, of his profession and of the world. He
had not the fire, the celerity, the genial cordiality of Sherman, whose person and manner emit-
ted a *ray* (to adopt, with a very slight change,
Lamb's well-known lines) —

"a ray
Which struck a cheer upon the day,
A cheer which would not go away—"

Grant had not these. But he certainly had a good deal of the character and qualities which we so justly respect in the Duke of Wellington. Wholly free from show, parade, and pomposity ; sensible and sagacious ; scanning closely the situation, seeing things as they actually were, then making up his mind as to the right thing to be done under the circumstances, and doing it ; never flurried, never vacillating, but also not stubborn, able to reconsider and change his plans, a man of resource ; when, however, he had really fixed on the best course to take, the right nail to drive, resolutely and tenaciously persevering, driving the nail hard home — Grant was all this, and surely in all this he resembles the Duke of Wellington.

The eyes of Europe, during the War of Secession, were chiefly fixed on the conflict in the East. Grant, however, as we have seen, began his career, not on the great and conspicuous stage of the East, but in the West. He did not come to the East until, by taking Vicksburg, he had attracted all eyes to the West, and to the course of events there.

We have seen how Grant's first expedition in command ended. The second ended in much the same way, and is related by him with the same humour. He was ordered to move against a Colonel Thomas Harris, encamped on the Salt River. As Grant and his men approached the place where they expected to find Harris, "my heart," he says, "kept getting higher and higher, until it felt to me as if it was in my throat." But when they reached the point from which they looked down into the valley where they supposed Harris to be, behold, Harris was gone! "My heart resumed its place. It occurred to me at once that Harris had been as much afraid of me as I had been of him. This was a view of the question I had never taken before, but I never forgot it afterwards. I never forgot that an enemy had as much reason to fear my forces as I had his. The lesson was valuable."

But already he inspired confidence. Shortly after his return from the Salt River, the President asked the Congressmen from Illinois to recommend seven citizens of that State for the rank of brigadier-general, and the Congressmen unanimously recommended Grant first on the list. In August he was appointed to the command of a district, and on the 4th of September assumed command at Cairo, where the Ohio River joins the Mississippi. His first important success was to seize and fortify Paducah, an important post at the mouth of the Tennessee River, about fifty miles from Cairo. By the 1st of November he had 20,000 well-drilled men under his command. In November he fought a smart action at Belmont, on the western bank of the Mississippi, with the object of preventing the Confederates who were in strong force at Columbus in Kentucky, on the eastern bank, from detaching troops to the West. He succeeded in his object, and his troops, who came under fire for the first time, behaved well. Grant himself had a horse shot under him.

Very important posts to the Confederates were Fort Henry on the Tennessee and Fort Donelson on the Cumberland River. Grant thought he could capture Fort Henry. He went to St. Louis to see General Halleck, whose subordinate he was, and to state his plan. "I was received with so little cordiality that I perhaps stated the object of my visit with less clearness than I might have done, and I had not uttered many sentences before I was cut short as if my plan was preposterous. I returned to Cairo very much crest-fallen."

He persevered, however, and after consulting with the officer commanding the gunboats at Cairo, he renewed, by telegraph, the suggestion that, if permitted, he "could take and hold Fort Henry on the Tennessee." This time he was backed by the officer in command of the

gunboats.   Next day, he wrote fully to explain
his plan.   In two days he received instructions
from headquarters to move upon Fort Henry,
and on the 2nd of February, 1862, the expedition started.

He took Fort Henry on the 6th of February,
and announcing his success to General Halleck,
informed him that he would now take Fort Donelson.   On the 16th, Fort Donelson surrendered,
and Grant made nearly 15,000 prisoners.   There
was delight in the North, depression at Richmond.   Grant was at once promoted to be
major-general of volunteers.   He thought, both
then and ever after, that by the fall of Fort
Donelson the way was opened to the forces of
the North all over the south-west without
much resistance, that a vigorous commander,
disposing of all the troops west of the Alleghanies, might have at once marched to Chattanooga, Corinth, Memphis, and Vicksburg, and
broken down every resistance.   There was no
such commander, and time was given to the
enemy to collect armies and fortify new positions.

The next point for attack was Corinth, at the
junction of the two most important railroads in
the Mississippi Valley.   After Grant had, after
a hard and bloody struggle of two days, won

the battle of Shiloah, in which a ball cut in two the scabbard of his sword, and more than 10,000 men were killed and wounded on the side of the North, General Halleck, who did not love Grant, arrived on the scene of action and assumed the command. "Although next to him in rank," says Grant, "and nominally in command of my old district and army, I was ignored as much as if I had been at the most distant point of territory within my jurisdiction." On the advance to Corinth, "I was little more than an observer. Orders were sent direct to the right wing or reserve, ignoring me, and advances were made from one line of intrenchments to another without notifying me. My position was so embarrassing, in fact, that I made several applications to be relieved." When he suggested a movement, he was silenced. Presently the Confederate troops evacuated Corinth in safety, carrying with them all public property. On the side of the North, there was much disappointment at the slackness with which the enemy had been pressed, and at his success in saving his entire army.

But Corinth was evacuated; the naval forces of the North took Memphis, and now held the Mississippi River from its source to that point; New Orleans and Baton Rouge had

fallen into their possession.   The Confederates
at the West were now narrowed down, for als
communication with Richmond, to the single
line of road running east from Vicksburg.   To
dispossess them of Vicksburg, therefore, was of
the highest importance.   At this point I must
stop for the present.   Public attention was not
yet fixed upon Grant, as it became after his success at Vicksburg; and with his success there
a second chapter of his life opens.   But already
he had shown his talent for succeeding.   Car-
dinal Mazarin used to ask concerning a man
before employing him, *Est-il heureux?*   Grant
was *heureux.*

PART II.

WE left Grant projecting his attack upon Vicksburg. In the autumn of 1862, the second year of the war, the prospect for the North appeared gloomy. The Confederates were further advanced than at the beginning of the struggle. Many loyal people, says Grant, despaired at that time of ever saving the Union; President Lincoln never himself lost faith in the final triumph of the Northern cause, but the administration at Washington was uneasy and anxious. The elections of 1862 had gone against the party which was for prosecuting the war at all costs and at all risks until the Union was saved. Voluntary enlistments had ceased; to fill the ranks of the Northern armies the draft had been resorted to. Unless a great success came to restore the spirit of the North, it seemed probable that the draft would be resisted, that men would begin to desert, and that the power to capture and punish deserters would be lost. It was Grant's conviction that there was nothing left to be done but *"to go forward to a decisive victory."*

At first, however, after the battle of Shiloh
and the taking of Corinth, he could accomplish
little. General Halleck, his chief, appears to
have been at this time ill-disposed to him, and
to have treated him with coldness and incivility.
In July 1862, General Halleck was appointed
general-in-chief of all the armies of the North,
with his headquarters in Washington, and Grant
remained in Tennessee in chief command. But
his army suffered such depletion by detaching
men to defend long lines of communication, to
repair ruined railroads, to reinforce generals in
need of succour, that he found himself entirely
on the defensive in a hostile territory. Nevertheless in a battle fought to protect Corinth he
repulsed the enemy with great slaughter, and
being no longer anxious for the safety of the
territory within his command, and having been
reinforced, he resolved on a forward movement
against Vicksburg.

Vicksburg occupies the first high ground on
the Mississippi below Memphis. Communication between the parts of the Confederacy divid-
ed by the Mississippi was through Vicksburg,
So long as the Confederates held Vicksburg-
and Port Hudson lower down, the free naviga-
tion of the river was prevented. The fall of
Vicksburg, as the event proved, was sure to

bring with it the fall of Port Hudson also.
Grant saw nearly his whole force absorbed in
holding the railway lines north of Vicksburg;
he considered that if he moved forward, driving
the enemy before him into Southern territory
not as yet subdued, those lines in his rear would
almost hold themselves, and most of his force
would be free for field operations. But in moving forward he moved further from his bases of
supplies. One of these was at Holly Springs,
in the north of the state of Mississippi; the
enemy appeared there, captured the garrison,
and destroyed all the stores of food, forage, and
munitions of war. This loss taught Grant a
lesson by which he, and Sherman after him,
profited greatly: the lesson that in a wide and
productive country, such as that in which he
was operating, to cling to a distant base of
supply was not necessary; the country he was
in would afford the supplies needed. He was
amazed, he says, when he was compelled by the
loss of Holly Springs to collect supplies in the
country immediately around him, at the abundant
quantity which the country afforded. He found
that after leaving two months' supplies for the
use of the families whose stores were taken, he
could, off the region where he was, have sub-
sisted his army for a period four times as long

as he had actually to remain there. Later in
the campaign he took full advantage of the experience thus gained.

The fleet under Admiral Porter co-operated
with him, but all endeavours to capture Vicksburg from the north were unavailing. The
Mississippi winds and winds through its rich
alluvial valley; the country is intersected by
bayous or water-courses filled from the river,
with overhanging trees and with narrow and
tortuous channels, where the bends could not
be turned by a vessel of any length. To cross
this country in the face of an enemy was impossible. The problem was to get in rear of the
object of attack, and to secure a footing upon
dry ground on the high or eastern side of the
Mississippi—the side on which Vicksburg
stands—for operating against the place. On
the 30th of January, 1863, Grant having left
Memphis, took the command at Young's Point
in Louisiana, on the western bank of Mississippi,
not far above Vicksburg, bent on solving the
problem.

It was a wet country and a wet winter, with
high water in the Mississippi and its tributaries.
The troops encamped on the river bank had, in
order to be out of the water, to occupy the
levees, or dykes, along the river edge, and the

ground immediately behind. This gave so limited a space, that one corps of Grant's army, when he assumed the command at Young's Point, was at Lake Providence, seventy miles above Vicksburg. The troops suffered much from malarial fevers and other sickness, but the hospital arrangements were excellent.

Four ineffectual attempts were in the course of the winter made to get at the object of attack by various routes. Grant, meanwhile, was maturing his plan. His plan was to traverse the peninsula where he lay encamped, then to cross the Mississippi, and thus to be able to attack Vicksburg from the south and east. Above Young's Point, at Milliken's Bend, begins a series of bayous, forming, as it were, the chord of an immense bend of the Mississippi, and falling into the river some fifty miles below Vicksburg. Behind the levees bordering these bayous were tolerable roads, by which, as soon as they emerged from the waters, Grant's troops and waggon-trains could cross the peninsula. The difficulties were indeed great : four bridges had to be built across wide bayous, and the rapid fall of the waters increased the current, and made bridge-building troublesome ; but at work of this kind the " Yankee soldier " is in his element. By the 24th of April Grant had his headquarters at the southern extremity of the bend. The navy under Admiral Porter, escorting steamers and barges to serve as ferries and for the transport of supplies, had run fourteen miles of batteries, passed Vicksburg, and come down the river to join Grant. A further march of twenty-two miles was still necessary in order to reach the first high ground, where the army might land and establish itself on the eastern shore. This first high land is at Grand Gulf, a place strongly held at that time by the Confederates, and as unattackable from the river as Vicksburg itself. Porter ran the batteries of Grand Gulf as he had run those of Vicksburg; the army descended the river a few miles, and on the 30th of April was landed at Bruinsburg, on the eastern shore, without meeting an enemy.

Grant's plan had succeeded. He was established on the eastern bank, below and in rear of Vicksburg. Though Vicksburg was not yet taken, and though he was in the enemy's country, with a vast river and the stronghold of Vicksburg between him and his base of supplies, yet he "felt a degree of relief scarcely ever equalled, since I was on dry ground on the same side of the river with the enemy."

And indeed from this moment his success was continuous. The enemy had at Grand

Gulf, at Haines Bluff north of Vicksburg, and
at Jackson, the capital of the State of Mississippi, in which State all these places are, about
60,000 men. After fighting and losing an
action to cover Grand Gulf, the Confederates
evacuated that place, and Grant occupied it on
the 3rd of May. By the 7th of May Sherman
joined him at Grand Gulf, and he found himself with a force of 33,000 men. He then
determined at once to attack the enemy's
forces in the rear of Vicksburg, and then to
move on the stronghold itself. In order to use
Grand Gulf as his base of supplies for these
operations, he must have constructed additional roads, and this would have been a work
of time. He determined therefore merely to
bring up by the single road available from
Grand Gulf, what rations of biscuit, coffee,
and salt he could, and to make the country he
traversed furnish everything else. Beef, mut-
ton, poultry, molasses, and forage were to be
found, he knew, in abundance. The cautious
Halleck would be sure to disapprove this bold
plan of almost abandoning the base of supplies, but Grant counted on being able to ob-
tain his object before he could be interfered
with from Washington.

The nature of the ground making Vicksburg

easily defensible on the south, Grant determined to get on the railroad running east from
Vicksburg to Jackson, the State capital, and to
approach the stronghold from that side. At
Jackson was a strong Confederate force, the
city was an important railway centre, and all
supplies of men and stores for Vicksburg came
thence; this source of aid had to be stopped.
But in order to reach Jackson, Grant had to
abandon even that one road by which he had
partially supplied his army hitherto, to cut
loose from his base of supplies altogether. He
did so without hesitation. After a successful
action he entered Jackson on the 14th of May,
driving out of it the Confederates under General Johnston, and destroyed the place in so
far as it was a railroad centre and a manufactory of military supplies. Then he turned
westward, and after a severe battle shut up
Pemberton in Vicksburg. An assault on Pemberton's defences was unsuccessful, but Vicksburg was closely invested. Pemberton's stores
began to run short. Johnston was unable to
come to his relief, and on the 4th of July, Independence Day, he surrendered Vicksburg,
with its garrison of nearly thirty-two thousand
men, ordnance and stores. As Grant had fore-
seen, Port Hudson surrendered as soon as the

fall of Vicksburg became known, and the great river was once more open from St. Louis to the sea.

In the north the victory of Gettysburg was won on the same day on which Vicksburg surrendered. A load of anxiety was lifted from the minds of the President and his ministers; the North took heart again, and resolved to continue the war with energy, in the hope of soon bringing it to a triumphant issue. The great and decisive event bringing about this change was the fall of Vicksburg, and the merit of that important success was due to Grant.

He had been successful, and in his success he still retained his freedom from "bounce" and from personal vanity; his steadfast concern for the public good; his moderation. Let us hear his account of being under fire during a fruitless attack by Admiral Porter's gunboats on the batteries of Grand Gulf:

"I occupied a tug, from which I could see the effect of the battle on both sides, within range of the enemy's guns; *but a small tug, without armament, was not calculated to attract the fire of batteries while they were being assailed themselves.*"

He has to mention a risk incurred by himself; but mentioning it, he is at pains to minimise it.

When he assumed command in person at Young's Point, General McClernand, from whom the command now passed to Grant, his senior and superior, showed temper and remonstrated:

"His correspondence with me on the subject was more in the nature of a reprimand than a protest. It was highly insubordinate, *but I overlooked it, as I believed, for the good of the service.* General McClernand was a member of Congress when the Secession War broke out; he belonged to that party which furnished all the opposition there was to a vigorous prosecution of the war for saving the Union; but there was no delay in his declaring himself for the Union at all hazards, and there was no uncertain sound in his declaration of where he stood in the contest before the country."

To such a man Grant wished to be forbearing when he could say to himself that, after all, it was only his own dignity which was concerned. But later, when an irregularity of the same General was injurious to good feeling and unity in the army, Grant was prompt and severe:

"I received a letter from General Sherman, and one from General McPherson, saying that their respective commands had complained to

them of a fulsome congratulatory order published by General McClernand to the 13th
Corps, which did great injustice to the other
troops engaged in the campaign. This order
had been sent north and published, and now
papers containing it had reached our camps.
The order had not been heard of by me; I at
once wrote to McClernand, directing him to
send me a copy of this order. He did so, and I
at once relieved him from the command of the
13th Army Corps. The publication of his order
in the press was in violation of War Department
orders, and also of mine."

The newspaper press is apt to appear to an
American, even more than to an Englishman,
as part of the order of nature, and contending
with it seems like contending with destiny.
Grant had governing instincts. "I always ad-
mired the South, as bad as I thought their
cause, for the boldness with which they silenced
all opposition and all croaking by press or by
individuals within their control." His instincts
would have led him to follow this example.
But since he could do nothing against the newspaper nuisance, and was himself the chief suf-
ferer by it, he bore it with his native philosophy :

"Visitors to the camps went home with dismal

stories.   Northern papers came back to the soldiers with these stories exaggerated.   Because
I would not divulge my ultimate plans to visitors they pronounced me idle, incompetent, and
unfit to command men in an emergency, and
clamoured for my removal.   They were not
to be satisfied, many of them, with my simple
removal, but named who my successor should
be.   I took no steps to answer these complaints,
but continued to do my duty, as I understood
it, to the best of my ability."

Surely the Duke of Wellington would have
read these *Memoirs* with pleasure.   He might
himself have issued, too, this order respecting
behaviour to prisoners : "Instruct the commands to be quiet and orderly as these prisoners
pass, and to make no offensive remark."   And
this other, respecting behaviour in a conquored
enemy's country : "Impress upon the men the
importance of going through the State in an
orderly manner, abstaining from taking anything not absolutely necessary for their sub-
sistence while travelling.   They should try to
create as favourable an impression as possible
upon the people."

But what even at this stage of the war is very
striking, and of good augury for the re-union
which followed, is the absence, in general, of

bitter hatred between the combatants. There is nothing of internecine, inextinguishable, irreconcilable enmity, or of the temper, acts, and words which beget this. Often we find the vanquished Southerner showing a good-humoured audacity, the victorious Northerner a good-humoured forbearance. Let us remember Carrier at Nantes, or Davoust at Hamburg, and then look at Grant's picture of himself and Sherman at Jackson, when their troops had just driven the enemy out of this capital of a "rebel" State, and were destroying the stores and war-materials there :

"Sherman and I went together into a manufactory which had not ceased work on account of the battle, nor for the entrance of Yankee troops. Our entrance did not seem to attract the attention of either the manager or the operatives, most of whom were girls. We looked on for a while to see the tent cloth which they were making roll out of the looms, with "C.S. A."* woven in each bolt. Finally I told Sherman I thought they had done work enough. The operatives were told they could leave, and take with them what cloth they could carry. In a few minutes the factory was in a blaze. The proprietor visited Washington, while I was Presi-

* Confederate States Army.

dent, to get his pay for this property, claiming
that it was private."

The American girls coolly continuing to make
the Confederate tents under the eye of the hostile generals, and the proprietor claiming afterwards to be paid by Congress for them as private
property, are charming.

It was one of Grant's superstitions, he tells
us, never to apply for a post, or to use personal
or political influence for obtaining it. He believed that if he had got it in this way he would
have feared to undertake any plan of his own
conception for fear of involving his patrons in
responsibility for his possible failure. If he
were selected for a post, his responsibility ended,
he said, with "his doing the best he knew how.'

"Every one has his superstitions. One of
mine is that in positions of great responsibility
every one should do his duty to the best of his
ability, where assigned by competent authority,
without application or the use of influence to
change his position. While at Cairo I had
watched with very great interest the operations
of the Army of the Potomac, looking upon that
as the main field of the war. I had no idea, myself, of ever having any large command, nor did I
suppose that I was equal to one; but I had the
vanity to think that, as a cavalry officer, I might

succeed very well in the command of a brigade. On one occasion, in talking about this to my staff officers, I said that I would give anything if I were commanding a brigade of cavalry in the Army of the Potomac, and I believed I could do some good. Captain Hellyer suggested that I should make application to be transferred there to command the cavalry. I then told him that I would cut my right arm off first, and mentioned this superstition."

But now he was to be transferred, without any solicitation on his own part, to "the main field of the war." At first, however, he was appointed to the command of the "Military Division of the Mississippi," and after fighting a severe and successful battle at Chattanooga in November (1863), relieved that place and Knoxville, which the Confederates were threatening. President Lincoln, who had daily, almost hourly, been telegraphing to him to "remember Burnside," to "do something for Burnside," besieged in Knoxville, was overjoyed. " I wish," he wrote to Grant, "to tender you, and all under your command, my more than thanks, my profoundest gratitude, for the skill, courage and perseverance with which you and they, over so great difficulties, have effected this important object. God bless you all!" Congress voted him thanks and a gold medal for his achievements at Vicksburg and Chattanooga.

In the dead of the winter, with the thermometer below zero, he made an excursion into Kentucky, and had the pleasure of finding the people along his route, both in Tennessee and Kentucky, in general intensely loyal to the Union :

" They would collect in little places where we would stop of evenings, to see me. The people naturally expected to see the commanding general the oldest person in the party. I was then forty-one years of age, while my medical director was grey-haired, and probably twelve or more years my senior. The crowds would generally swarm around him, and thus give me an opportunity of quietly dismounting and getting into the house."

At the beginning of the next year, 1864, a Bill was passed through Congress for restoring the grade of Lieutenant-General in the army. Grant was nominated to that rank, and having been summoned to Washington he received his commission from the President on the 9th of March, in the presence of the Ministers. Before he came to Washington, he had meant to return to his command in the West even after being made lieutenant-general; but at Washington he saw reason to change his mind. The important struggle was now between the Army of the Potomac and Lee. From what he saw, Grant was convinced that in that struggle no one except himself, with the superior rank he now bore, could, probably, "resist the pressure that would be brought to bear upon him to desist from his own plans and pursue others." He obtained, therefore, the nomination of Sherman to succeed him in command of the Military Division of the Mississippi. On the 12th of March orders were published by the War Department, placing Grant in chief command of all the armies.

The position of General Meade, who was at that time in command of the Army of the Potomac, and who had won the important battle of Gettysburg in the previous summer, underwent a grave change through Grant's promotion. Both Meade and Grant behaved very well. Meade suggested to Grant that he might wish to have immediately under him Sherman, who had been serving with Grant in the West. He begged him not to hesitate in making the change if he thought it for the good of the service. The work in hand, he said, was of such vast importance, that the feelings and wishes of no one person should stand in the way of select-

ing the right men. He was willing himself to
serve to the best of his ability wherever placed.
Grant assured him that he had no thought of
moving him, and in his *Memoirs*, after relating
what had passed, he adds : " This incident gave
me even a more favorable opinion of Meade than
did his great victory at Gettysburg the July
before. It is men who wait to be selected,
and not those who seek, from whom we may
always expect the most efficient service." He
tried to make Meade's position as nearly as possible what it would have been had he himself
been away in Washington or elsewhere ; he
gave all orders for the movements of the Army
of the Potomac to Meade for execution, and to
avoid the necessity of having to give direct
orders himself, he established his headquarters
close to Meade's whenever he could. Meade's
position, however, was undoubtedly a somewhat
embarrassing one ; but its embarrassment was
not increased by soreness on his part, or by
want of delicacy on Grant's.

In the West, the great objects to be attained
by Sherman were the defeat of Johnston and
his army, and the occupation of Atlanta. These
objects he accomplished, proceeding afterwards
to execute his brilliant and famous march to
Savannah and the sea, sweeping the whole

State of Georgia. In the East, the opposing forces stood between the Federal and Confederate capitals, and substantially in the same relations to each other as when the war began three years before. President Lincoln told Grant, when he first saw him in private, that although he had never professed to know how campaigns should be conducted, and never wanted to interfere in them, yet "procrastination on the part of commanders, and the pressure from the people at the North and Congress, *which was always with him*, forced him into issuing his series of Military Orders. He did not know but they were all wrong, and did know that some of them were. What he wanted," he continued, "was a general who would take the responsibility and act; he would support him with all the power of the Government." He added that he did not even ask to know what Grant's plans were. But such is human nature, that the next moment he brought out a map of Virginia, showed Grant two streams running into the Potomac, and suggested a plan of his own for landing the army between the mouths of these streams, which would protect its flanks while it moved out. "I listened respectfully," says Grant, with dry humour, "but did not suggest that the same streams would protect Lee's flanks while he was shutting us up."

In Grant the President had certainly found a general who would take the responsibility, would act, and would keep his plans to himself. To beat Lee and get possession of his army, was the object. If Lee was beaten and his army captured, the fall of Richmond must necessarily follow. If Richmond were taken by moving the army thither on transports up the James River, but meanwhile Lee's army were to remain whole and unimpaired, the end of the war was not brought any nearer. But the end of the war must be reached soon, or the North might grow weary of continuing the struggle. For three years the war had raged, with immense losses on either side, and no decisive consummation reached by either. If the South could succeed in prolonging an indecisive struggle year after year still, the North might probably grow tired of the contest, and agree to a separation. Persuaded of this, Grant, at the beginning of May 1864, crossed the Rapidan with the Army of the Potomac, and commenced the forty-three days' Campaign of the Wilderness.

The Wilderness is a tract north of Richmond, between the Rapidan and the James River, much cut up with streams and morasses, full of broken ground, densely clothed with wood, and thinly inhabited. The principal streams between the Rapidan and the James River are the branches of the Anna, uniting in the Pamunkey, and the Chickahominy. The coun-try was favorable for defence, and Lee was a general to make the most of its advantages. Grant was in an enemy's country, but, moving by his left flank, was in connection with the sea, of which the Northerners were masters, and was abundantly supplied with everything. Of artillery, in particular, he had so much that he was embarrassed by it, and had to send some of it away. Overwhelmingly superior in num-bers and resources, he pressed steadily forward, failing and repulsed sometimes, but coolly per-severing. This campaign, of which the stages are the battles of Chancellorsville, Spottsyl-vania, North Anna and Cold Harbour, was watched at the time in Europe with keen at-tention, and is much better known than the operations in the West. I shall not attempt any account of it; for its severity let the losses of Grant's successful army speak. When he crossed the Rapidan the Army of the Potomac numbered 115,000 men; during the forty-three days' campaign reinforcements were received amounting to 40,000 men more. When the army crossed the James River, it was 116,000 strong, almost exactly the same strength as at the beginning of the campaign. Thirty-nine thousand men had been lost in forty-three days.

A yet greater loss must have been incurred had Grant attacked Lee's lines in front of Richmond; and therefore crossing the James River, he invested, after failing to carry it by assault, Petersburg, the enemy's important stronghold south of Richmond. Winter came and passed. Lee's army was safe in its lines, and Richmond had not yet fallen; but the Confederates' resources were failing, their foes gathering, and the end came visibly near. After sweeping Georgia and taking Savannah in December, Sherman turned north and swept the Carolinas, ready to join with Grant in moving upon Lee in the spring. Sheridan made himself master of the Shenandoah Valley, and closed to the Confederates that great source of supply. Finally Grant, resuming operations in March 1865, possessed himself of the outer works of Petersburg, and of the railroad by which the place was supplied from the southwest, and on the 3rd of April Petersburg was evacuated. Then Grant proceeded to possess himself of the railroad by which Lee's army and Richmond itself now drew their supplies. Lee had already informed his government that he could hold out no longer. The Confederate President was at church when the despatch arrived, the congregation were told that there would be no evening service, and the authorities abandoned Richmond that afternoon. In the field there was some sharp fighting for a day or two still; but Lee's army was crumbling away, and on the 9th of April he wrote to Grant, requesting an interview with him for the purpose of surrendering his army. Grant was suffering from sick headache when the officer bearing Lee's note reached him, "but the instant I saw," he says, "the contents of the note, I was cured."

Then followed, in the afternoon of that same day, the famous interview at Appomattox Court House. Grant shall himself describe the meeting:

"When I had left camp that morning I had not expected so soon the result that was then taking place, and consequently was in rough garb. I was without a sword, as I usually was when on horseback in the field, and wore a soldier's blouse for a coat, with the shoulder-straps of my rank to indicate to the army who I was.

When I went into the house I found General Lee. We greeted each other, and, after shaking hands, took our seats.

"What General Lee's feelings were I do not know. As he was a man of much dignity, with an impassible face, it was impossible to say whether he felt inwardly glad that the end had finally come, or felt sad over the result and was too manly to show it. Whatever his feelings, they were entirely concealed from my observation; but my own feelings, which had been quite jubilant on the receipt of his letter, were sad and depressed. I felt like anything rather than rejoicing at the downfall of a foe who had fought so long and valiantly, and had suffered so much for a cause, though that cause was, I believe, one of the worst for which a people ever fought.

"General Lee was dressed in a full uniform which was entirely new, and was wearing a sword of considerable value, very likely the sword which had been presented by the State of Virginia. In my rough travelling suit, the uniform of a private with the straps of a lieutenant-general, I must have contrasted very strangely with a man so handsomely dressed, six feet high and of faultless form. But this was not a matter that I thought of until afterwards.

"We soon fell into a conversation about old army times. He remarked that he remembered me well in the old army (of Mexico) ; and I told him that as a matter of course I remembered *him* perfectly, but from the difference in our rank and years (there being about sixteen years' difference in our ages) I had thought it likely that I had not attracted his attention sufficiently to be remembered by him after such a long interval. Our conversation grew so pleasant that I almost forgot the object of our meeting. After the conversation had run on in this style for some time, General Lee called my attention to the object of our meeting, and said that he had asked for this interview for the purpose of getting from me the terms I proposed to give his army. I said that I meant merely that his army should lay down their arms, not to take them up again during the continuance of the war unless duly and properly exchanged."

Lee acquiesced, and Grant, who throughout the interview seems to have behaved with true delicacy and kindness, proceeded to write out the terms of surrender. It occurred to him, as he was writing, that it would be an unnecessary humiliation to the officers to call upon them to surrender their side-arms, and also that they would be glad to retain their private horses and effects, and accordingly he inserted in the terms that the surrender of arms and property was not to include the side-arms, horses and property of the officers. Lee remarked that this would have a happy effect on the army. Grant then said that most of the men in Lee's ranks were, he supposed, small farmers; that the country had been so raided by either army that it was doubtful whether they would be able to put in a crop to carry themselves and their families through the next winter without the aid of the horses they were then riding; that the United States did not want them, and he would therefore give instructions to let every man of the Confederate army, who claimed to own a horse or mule, take the animal to his home. Again Lee remarked that this would have a happy effect.

At half-past four Grant could telegraph to the Secretary of War at Washington: "General Lee surrendered the army of Northern Virginia this afternoon." As soon as the news of the surrender became known, Grant's army began to fire a salute of a hundred guns. Grant instantly stopped it.

The war was at an end. Johnston surrendered to Sherman in North Carolina. President Lincoln visited Richmond, which had been occupied by the Army of the Potomac the day after the Confederate Government abandoned it. The President on his return to Washington invited Grant, who also had now gone thither, to accompany him to the theatre on the evening of the 14th of April. Grant declined, because he was to go off that evening to visit his children who were at school in New Jersey; when he reached Philadelphia, he heard that the President and Mr. Seward had been assassinated. He immediately returned to Washington, to find the joy there turned to mourning. With this tragic event, and with the grand review in the following month of Meade's and Sherman's armies by the new President, Mr. Johnson, the *Memoirs* end.

Modest for himself, Grant is boastful, as Americans are apt to be, for his nation. He says with perfect truth that troops who have fought a few battles and won, and followed up their victories, improve upon what they were before to an extent that can hardly be counted by percentage; and that his troops and Sherman's which had gone through this training, were by the end of the war become very good and seasoned soldiers. But he is fond of adding, in what I must call the American vein,

"*better than any European soldiers.*" And the
reason assigned for this boast is in the American vein too: "Because they not only worked
like a machine, but the machine thought. European armies know very little what they are
fighting for, and care less." Is the German
army a machine which does not think? Did
the French revolutionary armies know very
little what they were fighting for, and care
less? Sainte-Beuve says charmingly that he
"cannot bear to have it said that he is the *first*
in anything; it is not a thing that can be admitted, and these ways of classing people
give offence." German military men read
Grant's boast, and are provoked into replying
that the campaigns and battles of the American Civil War were mere struggles of militia;
English military men say that Americans have
been steady enough behind breastworks and
entrenchments against regulars, but never in
the open field. Why cannot the Americans,
in speaking of their nation, take Sainte-Beuve's
happy and wise caution?

The point is worth insisting on, because to be
always seeking to institute comparisons, and
comparisons to the advantage of their own country, is with so many Americans a *tic*, a mania,
which every one notices in them, and which

sometimes drives their friends half to despair. Recent greatness is always apt to be sensitive and self-assertive; let us remember Dr. Hermann Grimm on Goethe. German literature, as a power, does not begin before Lessing; if Germany had possessed a great literature for six centuries, with names in it like Dante, Montaigne, Shakespeare, probably Dr. Hermann Grimm would not have thought it necessary to call Goethe the greatest poet that has ever lived. But the Americans in the rage for comparison-making beat the world. Whatever excellence is mentioned, America must, if possible, be brought in to balance or surpass it. That fine and delicate naturalist, Mr. Burroughs, mentions trout, and instantly he adds : " British trout, by the way, are not so beautiful as our own; they are less brilliantly marked and have much coarser scales, there is no gold or vermilion in their colouring." Here superiority is claimed; if there is not superiority there must be at least balance. Therefore in literature we have "the American Walter Scott," the " American Wordsworth"; nay, I see advertised *The Primer of American Literature.* Imagine the face of Philip or Alexander at hearing of a Primer of Macedonian Literature ! Are we to have a Primer of Canadian Literature too, and

a Primer of Australian ?   We are all contribu-
tories to one great literature — English Literature.   The contribution of Scotland to this
literature is far more serious and important than
that of America has yet had time to be ; yet a
" Primer of Scotch Literature" would be an
absurdity.   And these things are not only absurd ; they are also retarding.

My opinion on any military subject is of
course worth very little, but I should have
thought that in what Napier calls "strength
and majesty " as a fighter, the American soldier,
if we are to institute these comparisons, had his
superiors ; though as brave as any one, he is too
ingenious, too mental, to be the perfection of a
fighting animal.   Where the Yankee soldier has
an unrivalled advantage is in his versatility and
ingenuity ; dexterous, willing, suggestive, he
can turn his hand to anything, and is of twenty
trades at the same time with that of soldier.
Grant's *Memoirs* are full of proofs of this faculty,
which might perhaps be of no great use in a
campaign in the Low Countries, but was invaluable in such campaigns as those which Grant and
Sherman conducted in America.   When the batteries at Vicksburg were to be run with hired
river steamers, there were naturally but very few
masters or crews who were willing to accompany

their vessels on this service of danger. Volunteers were therefore called for from the army,
men who had any experience in river naviga-
gation. "Captains, pilots, mates, engineers, and
deck-hands, enough presented themselves," says
Grant, "to take five times the number of vessels we were moving." The resource and
rapidity shown by the troops in the repair of
railroads wrecked by the enemy were marvellous.
In Sherman's Atlanta campaign, the Confederate cavalry lurking in his rear to burn bridges
and obstruct his communications had become so
disgusted at hearing trains go whistling by,
within a few hours after a bridge had been
burned, that they proposed to try blowing up
some of the tunnels. One of them said on this :
"No use, boys ; old Sherman carries duplicate
tunnels with him, and will replace them as fast
as you can blow them up ; better save your
powder !"

But a leader to use these capable and intelligent forces, to use all the vast resources of
the North, was needed, a leader wise, cool, firm,
bold, persevering, and at the same time, as Car-
dinal Mazarin says, *heureux ;* and such a leader
the United States found in General Grant.

He concludes his *Memoirs* by some advice to
his own country and some remarks on ours.

The United States, he says, are going on as if in the greatest security, "when they have not the power to resist an invasion by the fleets of fourth-rate European Powers for a time until we could prepare for them." The United States "should have a good navy, and our sea-coast defences should be put in the finest possible condition. Neither of these cost much when it is considered where the money goes and what we get in return."

The tone and temper of his remarks on England, and on her behaviour during the war, are in honourable contrast with the angry acrimony shown by many who should have known better. He regretted, he said, the exasperation. "The hostility of England to the United States, during our rebellion, was not so much real as it was apparent. It was the hostility of the leaders of one political party. England and the United States are natural allies, and should be the best of friends."

The *Memoirs* stop, as I have said, in 1865, and do not embrace Grant's Presidency, his journey to Europe, his financial disaster, his painful illness and death. As to his financial disaster, I will repeat what one of Grant's best friends, a man of great business faculty and of great fortune, remarked to me. I had been

saying, what one says so easily, that it was a
pity Grant had suffered himself to be drawn in
by speculators. "Yes," answered his friend,
"it was a pity. But see how it happened, and
put yourself in Grant's place. Like Grant, you
may have a son to whom you are partial, and
like Grant, you have no knowledge of business.
Had you been, like Grant, in a position to make
it worth while for a leader in business and
finance to come to you, saying that your son had
a quite exceptional talent for these matters, that
it was a thousand pities his talent should be
thrown away, 'give him to me and I will make
a man of him,' would you not have been flattered
in your parental pride, would you not have
yielded? This is what happened to Grant, and
all his financial misfortunes flowed from hence."
I listened, and could not deny that most probably I should have been flattered to my ruin, as
Grant was.

Grant's *Memoirs* are a mine of interesting
things; I have but scratched the surface and
presented a few samples. When I began, I did
not know that the book had been reprinted in
England; I find that it has,* and that its circulation here, though trifling indeed compared to
that in America, has been larger than I sup-

* By Messrs. Sampson Low, Marston & Co.,

posed. But certainly the book has not been read here anything like so much as it deserves. It contains a gallery of portraits, characters of generals who served in the war, for which alone the book, if it contained nothing else, would be well worth reading. But after all, its great value is in the character which, quite simply and unconsciously, it draws of Grant himself. The Americans are too self-laudatory, too apt to force the tone and thereby, as Sainte-Beuve says, to give offence; the best way for them to make us forgive and forget this is to produce what is simple and sterling. Instead of Primers of American Literature, let them bring forth more Maxims of Poor Richard; instead of assurances that they are "the greatest nation upon earth," let them give us more Lees, Lincolns, Shermans, and Grants.

MATTHEW ARNOLD.

A WORD ABOUT AMERICA.

II.

A WORD ABOUT AMERICA.

MR. LOWELL, in an interesting but rather
tart essay, "On a certain Condescension in
Foreigners," warns off Englishmen who may be
disposed to write or speak about the United
States of America. "I never blamed England
for not wishing well to democracy," he cries;
"how should she?" But the criticisms and
dealings of Englishmen, in regard to the object
of their ill-will, are apt, Mr. Lowell declares, to
make him impatient. "Let them give up trying
to understand us, still more thinking that they
do, and acting in various absurd ways as the
necessary consequence; for they will never
arrive at that devoutly to be wished consummation, till they learn to look at us as we are,
and not as they suppose us to be."

On the other hand, from some quarters in
America come reproaches to us for not speaking
about America enough, for not making sufficient
use of her in illustration of what we bring forward. Mr. Higginson expresses much surprise

that when, for instance, I dilate on the benefits of equality, it is to France that I have recourse for the illustration and confirmation of my thesis, not to the United States. A Boston newspaper supposes me to "speak of American manners as vulgar," and finds, what is worse, that the *Atlantic Monthly*, commenting on this supposed utterance of mine, adopts it and carries it further. For the writer in the *Atlantic Monthly* says that, indeed, "the hideousness and vulgarity of American manners are undeniable," and that "redemption is only to be expected by the work of a few enthusiastic individuals, conscious of cultivated tastes and generous desires"; or, as these enthusiasts are presently called by the writer, "rather highly civilized individuals, a few in each of our great cities and their environs." The Boston newspaper observes, with a good deal of point, that it is from these exceptional enthusiasts that the heroes of the tales of Mr. James and Mr. Howells seem to be recruited. It shrewdly describes them as "people who spend more than half their life in Europe, and return only to scold their agents for the smallness of their remittances"; and protests that such people "will have, and can have, no perceptible influence for good on the real civilization of Amer-

ica." Then our Boston friend turns to me
again, says that "it is vulgar people from the
large cities who have given Mr. Arnold his
dislike of American manners," and adds, that
"if it should ever happen that hard destiny
should force Mr. Arnold to cross the Atlantic,"
I should find "in the smaller cities of the interior, in the northern, middle, and southwestern
states, an elegant and simple social order, as
entirely unknown in England, Germany, or
Italy, as the private life of the dukes or princes
of the blood is unknown in America." Yes, I
"should find a manner of life belonging to the
highest civilization, in towns, in counties, and
in states whose names had never been heard" by
me ; and, if I could take the writer in the *Atlantic Monthly* to see it along with me, it would
do him, says his compatriot, a great deal of
good.

I do not remember to have anywhere, in
my too numerous writings, spoken of American
manners as vulgar, or to have expressed my
dislike of them. I have long accustomed myself
to regard the people of the United States as
just the same people with ourselves, as simply
"the English on the other side of the Atlantic."
The ethnology of that American diplomatist,
who the other day assured a Berlin audience

that the great admixture of Germans had now
made the people of the United States as much
German as English, has not yet prevailed with
me.   I adhere to my old persuasion, the Americans of the United States are English people
on the other side of the Atlantic.   I learned it
from Burke.   But from Burke I learned, too, with
what immense consequences and effects this
simple matter — the settlement of a branch of
the English people on the other side of the Atlantic — was, from the time of their constitution as an independent power, certainly and
inevitably charged.   Let me quote his own
impressive and profound words on the acknowl-
edgment of American independence, in 1782 : —

A great revolution has happened — a revolution made,
not by chopping and changing of power in any of the existing states, but by the appearance of a new state, of a
new species, in a new part of the globe.   It has made as
great a change in all the relations, and balances, and
gravitations of power, as the appearance of a new planet
would in the system of the solar world.

As for my esteeming it a hard destiny which
should force me to visit the United States, I will
borrow Goethe's words, and say, that " not the
spirit is bound, but the foot " ; with the best
will in the world, I have never yet been able to

go to America, and probably I never shall be able. But many a kind communication I receive from that quarter; and when one has much discoursed on equality and on civilization, and then is told that in America a lover of these will find just what suits him, and is invited, and almost challenged, to turn one's eyes there, and to bear testimony to what one beholds, it seems ungracious or cowardly to take no notice at all of such challenges, but to go on talking of equality and civilization just as if America had never existed. True, there is Mr. Lowell's warning. Englishmen easily may fall into absurdities in criticising America, most easily of all when they do not, and cannot, see it with their own eyes, but have to speak of it from what they read. Then, too, people are sensitive; certainly, it would be safer and pleasanter to say nothing. And as the prophet Jonah, when he had a message for Nineveh, hurried off in alarm down to Joppa, and incontinently took ship there for Tarshish, in just the opposite direction, so one might find plenty of reasons for running away from the task, when one is summoned to give one's opinion of American civilization. But Ewald says that it was a sorry and unworthy calculation, petty human reason-mongering — *menschliche Vernünftelei* — which

made Jonah run away from his task in this
fashion; and we will not run away from ours,
difficult though it be.

Besides, there are considerations which diminish its difficulty. When one has confessed the
belief that the social system of one's own
country is so far from being perfect that it presents us with the spectacle of an upper class
materialized, a middle class vulgarized, a lower
class brutalized, one has earned the right, perhaps, to speak with candor of the social systems
of other countries. Mr. Lowell complains that
we English make our narrow Anglicism, as he
calls it, the standard of all things; but "we are
worth nothing," says Mr. Lowell of himself
and his countrymen, "we are worth nothing
except so far as we have disinfected ourselves
of Anglicism." Mr. Hussey Vivian, the member for Glamorganshire, goes to travel in America, and when he comes back, delighted with
the country and the people, he publishes his
opinion that just two things are wanting to
their happiness, — a sovereign of the British
type, and a House of Lords : —

If Americans could only get over the first wrench, and
elect a king of the old stock, under the same limited con-
stitutional conditions as our sovereigns, and weld their
separate states into one compact and solid nation, many

of them would be only too thankful. I cannot help sus-
pecting, also, that they would not be sorry to transform
their Senate into a House of Lords. There are fortunes
amply large enough to support hereditary rule, and men
who will not now enter political life upon any consideration
would doubtless do their duty as patriotically as our peers,
if not compelled to face the dirt of candidature. As to
aristocratic ideas being foreign to Americans, I do not
believe it for a moment; on the contrary, I believe them
to be a highly aristocratic people.

I suppose this may serve as a specimen of the
Anglicism which is so exasperating to Mr. Lowell. I do not share it. Mr. Hussey Vivian has
a keen eye for the geological and mining facts
of America, but as to the political facts of that
country, the real tendencies of its life, and its
future, he does not seem to me to be at all at
the centre of the situation. Far from "not
wishing well to democracy," far from thinking
a king and a House of Lords, of our English
pattern, a panacea for social ills, I have freely
said that our system here, in my opinion, has
too much thrown the middle classes in upon
themselves, that the lower classes likewise are
thus too much thrown in upon themselves, and
that we suffer from the want of equality.
Nothing would please me better than to find
the difficulty solved in America, to find democracy a success there, with a type of equality

producing such good results, that, when one preaches equality, one should illustrate its advantages not from the example of the French, but, as Mr. Higginson recommends, from the example of the people of the United States. I go back again to my Boston newspaper:—

In towns whose names Mr. Arnold never heard, and never will hear, there will be found almost invariably a group of people of good taste, good manners, good education, and of self-respect, peers of any people in the world. Such people read the best books, they interpret the best music, they are interested in themes world-wide, and they meet each other with that mutual courtesy and that self-respect which belong to men and women who are sure of their footing.

This is what we want; and if American democracy gives this, Mr. Lowell may rely upon it that no narrow Anglicism shall prevent my doing homage to American democracy.

Only, we must have a clear understanding about one thing. This is a case where the question of numbers is of capital importance. Even in our poor old country, with its aristocratic class materialized, its middle class vulgarized, its lower class brutalized, there are to be found individuals, as I have again and again said, lovers of the humane life, lovers of perfection, who emerge in all classes, and who, while

they are more or less in conflict with the present, point to a better future. Individuals of
this kind I make no doubt at all that there are
in American society as well as here. The
writer in the *Atlantic Monthly* himself, unfavorable as is his judgment on his country's civilization in general, admits that he can find a certain
number of "enthusiastic individuals conscious
of cultivated tastes and generous desires." Of
these "rather highly civilized individuals" there
are, he says, "a few in each of our great cities
and their environs." His rebuker in the Boston
newspaper says that these centres of sweetness
and light are rather in the small towns than in
the large ones ; but that is not a matter of much
importance to us. The important question is :
In what numbers are they to be found ? Well,
there is *a group* of them, says the Boston newspaper, in almost any small town of the northern,
middle, and southwestern states. This is indeed civilization. A group of lovers of the
humane life, an "elegant and simple social
order," as its describer calls it, existing in almost
every small town of the northern, middle, and
southwestern states of America, and this in
addition to circles in New York and other great
cities with "a social life as dignified, as elegant,
and as noble as any in the world"— all this

must needs leaven American society, and must surely, if we can take example from it, enable us to leaven and transform our own. Leaven American society it already does, we hear:—

It is such people who keep the whole sentiment of the land up to a high standard. While the few "rather highly civilized individuals" are hopping backwards and forwards over the Atlantic to learn what is the last keynote which a pinchbeck emperor has decided on, or what is the last gore which a man-milliner has decreed, these American gentlemen and ladies, in the dignity of their own homes, are making America. It is they who maintain the national credit, it is they who steadily improve the standard of national education. If Mr. Arnold should ever see them in their own homes, it is they who will show him what is the normal type of American manners.

Our Boston informant writes so crisply and smartly that one is unwilling to part with him. I can truly say that I would rather read him and quote him than join issue with him. He has seen America, and I have not. Perhaps things in America are as he says. I am sure I hope they are, for, as I have just said, I have been long convinced that English society has to transform itself, and long looking in vain for a model by which we might be guided and inspired in the bringing forth of our new civilization; and here is the model ready to hand. But I own

that hitherto I have thought that, as we in
England have to transform our civilization, so
America has hers still to make ; and that, though
her example and co-operation might, and probably would, be of the greatest value to us in the
future, yet they were not of much use to our
civilization now.   I remember, that when I first
read the Boston newspaper from which I have
been quoting, I was just fresh from the perusal
of one of the best of Mr. James's novels, " Rod-
erick Hudson."   That work carries us to one of
the "smaller cities of the interior," a city of
which, I own, I had never heard — the American Northampton.   Those who have read " Rod-
erick Hudson " will recollect, that in that part of
the story where the scene is laid at Northampton, there occurs a personage called Striker, an
auctioneer.   And when I came upon the Boston
newspaper's assurances that, in almost every
small town of the Union, I should find "an
elegant and simple social order," the comment
which rose to my lips was this : " I suspect
what I should find there, in great force, is
Striker."   Now Striker was a Philistine.

I have said somewhere or other that, whereas
our society in England distributes itself into
Barbarians, Philistines, and Populace, America
is just ourselves, with the Barbarians quite left

out, and the Populace nearly.   This would leave
the Philistines for the great bulk of the nation ;
a livelier sort of Philistines than our Philistine
middle class which made and peopled the
United States — a livelier sort of Philistine
than ours, and with the pressure and the false
ideal of our Barbarians taken away, but left all
the more to himself, and to have his full swing.
That this should be the case seemed to me
natural, and that it actually was the case, everything which I could hear and read about America tended to convince me.   And when my
Boston friend talks of the " elegant and simple
social order established in almost every small
town in America, and of the group, in each, of
people of good taste, good manners, good education and self-respect, peers of any people in
the world," I cannot help thinking that things
are not quite so bright as he paints them, and
so superior to anything of which we have experience elsewhere ; that he is mixing two impressions together, the impression of individuals
scattered over the country, real lovers of the
humane life, but not yet numerous enough or
united enough to produce much effect, and the
impression of groups of worthy respectable
people to be found in almost every small town
of the Union, people with many merits, but not

yet arrived at that true and happy goal of civilization, "an elegant and simple social order."

We, too, have groups of this kind everywhere,
and we know what they can do for us and what
they cannot do. It is easy to praise them, to
flatter them, to express unbounded satisfaction
with them, to speak as if they gave us all that
we needed. We have done so here in England.
These groups, with us, these serious and effective forces of our middle class, have been ex-
tolled as "that section of the community which
has astonished the world by its energy, enter-
prise, and self-reliance, which is continually
striking out new paths of industry and subdu-
ing the forces of nature, which has done all the
great things that have been done in all depart-
ments, and which supplies the mind, the will,
and the power for all the great and good things
that have still to be done." So cry the newspapers ; our great orators take up the same
strain. The middle-class doers of English
race, with their industry and religion, are the
salt of the earth. " The cities you have built,"
exclaims Mr. Bright, "the railroads you have
made, the manufactures you have produced,
the cargoes which freight the ships of the
greatest mercantile navy the world has ever
seen ! " There we have their industry. Then

comes the praise of their religion, their own
specially invented and indomitably maintained
form of religion. "Let a man consider," exclaims Mr. Bright again, "how much of what
there is free and good and great, and constantly
growing in what is good, in this country, is
owing to Nonconformist action. Look at the
churches and chapels it has reared over the
whole country; look at the schools it has
built; look at the ministers it has supported;
look at the Christian work which it has conducted. It would be well for the Nonconformists, especially for the young among them, that
they should look back to the history of their
fathers, and that they should learn from them
how much is due to truth and how much they
have sacrificed to conscience."

It is the groups of industrious, religious, and
unshakable Nonconformists in all the towns,
small and great, of England, whose praise is
here celebrated by Mr. Bright. But he has
an even more splendid tribute of praise for
their brethren of the very same stock, and sort,
and virtue, in America also. The great scale of
things in America powerfully impresses Mr.
Bright's imagination always; he loves to count
the prodigious number of acres of land there,
the prodigious number of bushels of wheat

raised. The voluntary principle, the principle of modern English Nonconformity, is on the same grand and impressive scale. "There is nothing which piety and zeal have ever offered on the face of the earth as a tribute to religion and religious purposes, equal to that which has been done by the voluntary principle among the people of the United States."

I cannot help thinking that my Boston informant mixes up, I say, the few lovers of perfection with the much more numerous representatives, serious, industrious, and in many ways admirable, of middle-class virtue ; and imagines that in almost every town of the United States there is a group of lovers of perfection, whereas the lovers of perfection are much less thickly sown than he supposes, but what there really is in almost every town is a group of representatives of middle-class virtue. And the fruits by which he knows his men, the effects which they achieve for the national life and civilization, are just the fruits, be it observed, which the representatives of middle-class virtue are capable of producing and produce for us here in England, too, and for the production of which we need not have recourse to an extraordinary supply of lovers of perfection. "It is such people," he says, " who keep the whole sentiment of the

land up to a high standard when war comes, or
rebellion." But this is just what the middle-
class virtue of our race is abundantly capable
of doing ; as Puritan England in the seventeenth
century, and the inheritors of the traditions of
Puritan England since, have signally shown.
" It is they who maintain the national credit, it
is they who steadily improve the standard of
national education." By national education our
informant means popular education ; and here,
too, we are still entirely within the pale of middle-class achievement. Both in England and in
America, the middle class is abundantly capable
of maintaining the national credit, and does
maintain it. It is abundantly capable of rec-
ognizing the duty of sending to school the children of the people; nay, of sending them also,
if possible, to a Sunday school, and to chapel or
church. True ; and yet, in England at any rate,
the middle class, with all its industry and with
all its religiousness, — the middle class well typi-
fied, as I long ago pointed out, by a certain Mr.
Smith, a secretary to an insurance company,
who " labored under the apprehension that he
would come to poverty and that he was eter-
nally lost," — the English middle class presents
us at this day, for our actual needs, and for
the purposes of national civilization, with a de-

fective type of religion, a narrow range of intellect and knowledge, a stunted sense of beauty,
a low standard of manners. For the building
up of human life, as men are now beginning to
see, there are needed not only the powers of
industry and conduct, but the power, also, of
intellect and knowledge, the power of beauty,
the power of social life and manners. And
that type of life of which our middle class in
England are in possession is one by which
neither the claims of intellect and knowledge
are satisfied, nor the claim of beauty, nor the
claims of social life and manners.

That which in England we call the middle
class is in America virtually the nation. It is
in America in great measure relieved, as I have
said, of what with us is our Populace, and it is
relieved of the pressure and false ideal of our
Barbarians. It is generally industrious and
religious, as our middle class. Its religion is
even less invaded, I believe, by the modern
spirit than the religion of our middle class. An
American of reputation as a man of science tells
me that he lives in a town of a hundred and
fifty thousand people, of whom there are not
fifty who do not imagine the first chapters of
Genesis to be exact history. Mr. Dale, of Bir-
mingham, found, he says, that "orthodox Chris-

tian people in America were less troubled by attacks on the orthodox creed than the like people in England. They seemed to feel sure of their ground and they showed no alarm." Public opinion requires public men to attend regularly some place of worship. The favorite denominations are those with which we are here familiar as the denominations of Protestant dissent; when Mr. Dale tells us of "the Baptists, not including the Free Will Baptists, Seventh Day Baptists, Six Principle Baptists, and some other minor sects," one might fancy oneself reading the list of the sects in *Whitaker's Almanack*. But in America this type of religion is not, as it is here, a subordinate type, it is the predominant and accepted one. Our Dissenting ministers think themselves in paradise when they visit America. In that universally religious country, the religious denomination which has by much the largest number of adherents is that, I believe, of Methodism originating in John Wesley, and which we know in this country as having for its standard of doctrine Mr. Wesley's fifty-three sermons and notes on the New Testament. I have a sincere admiration for Wesley, and a sincere esteem for the Wesleyan Methodist body in this country; I have seen much of it, and for many of its members my esteem is not only sincere but also affectionate. I know how one's religious connections and religious attachments are determined by the circumstances of one's birth and bringing up ; and probably, if I had been born and brought up among the Wesley-ans, I should never have left their body. But certainly I should have wished my children to leave it ; because to live with one's mind, in regard to a matter of absorbing importance as Wesleyans believe religion to be, to live with one's mind, as to a matter of this sort, fixed constantly upon a mind of the third order, such as was Mr. Wesley's, seems to me extremely trying and injurious for the minds of men in general. And people whose minds, in what is the chief concern of their lives, are thus con-stantly fixed upon a mind of the third order, are the staple of the population of the United States, in the small towns and country districts above all. Yet our Boston friend asks us to believe, that a population of which this is the staple can furnish what we cannot furnish, cer-tainly, in England, and what no country that I know of can at present furnish, — a group, in every small town throughout the land, of people of good taste, good manners, good education, peers of any people in the world, reading the

best books, interpreting the best music, and
interested in themes world-wide! Individuals
of this kind, America can doubtless furnish,
peers of any people in the world ; and in every
town, groups of people with excellent qualities,
like the representatives of middle-class industry
and virtue among ourselves. And a country
capable of furnishing such groups will be strong
and prosperous, and has much to be thankful
for ; but it must not take these groups for what
they are not, or imagine that having produced
them it possesses what it does not possess, or
has provided for wants which are in fact still
unprovided for.

"The arts have no chance in poor countries,"
says Mr. Lowell. "From sturdy father to
sturdy son, we have been making this continent
habitable for the weaker Old World breed that
has swarmed to it, during the last half-century."
This may be quite true, and the achievements
wrought in America by the middle-class industry, the middle-class energy and courage, the
middle-class religion of our English race, may
be full as much as we have any right to expect
up to the present time, and only a people of
great qualities could have produced them. But
this is not the question. The question is as to
the establishment in America, on any consider-

able scale, of a type of civilization combining all those powers which go to the building up of a truly human life — the power of intellect and knowledge, the power of beauty, the power of social life and manners, as well as the great power of conduct and religion, and the indispensable power of expansion. "Is it not the highest act of a republic," asks Mr. Lowell, "to make men of flesh and blood, and not the marble ideals of such?" Let us grant it. "Perhaps it is the collective, not the individual humanity," Mr. Lowell goes on, "that is to have a chance of nobler development among us." Most true, the well-being of the many, and not of individuals and classes solely, comes out more and more distinctly to us all as the object which we must pursue. Many are to be made partakers of well-being, of civilization and humanization; we must not forget it, and America, happily, is not likely to let us forget it. But the ideal of well-being, of civilization, of humanization, is not to be, on that account lowered and coarsened.

Now the New York *Nation* — a newspaper which I read regularly and with profit, a newspaper which is the best, so far as my experience goes, of all American newspapers, and one of the best newspapers anywhere — the New York

Nation had the other day some remarks on the
higher sort of education in America, and the
utility of it, which were very curious : —

In America (says the *Nation*) scarcely any man who
can afford it likes to refuse his son a college education
if the boy wants it ; but probably not one boy in one
thousand can say, five years after graduating, that he has
been helped by his college education in making his start
in life. It may have been never so useful to him as a
means of moral and intellectual culture, but it has not
helped to adapt him to the environment in which he has
to live and work ; or, in other words, to a world in which
not one man in a hundred thousand has either the manners or cultivation of a gentleman, or changes his shirt
more than once a week, or eats with a fork.

Now upon this remarkable declaration many
comments might be made, but I am going now
to make one comment only. Is it credible, if
there were established in almost every town of
the great majority of the United States a type
of " elegant and simple social order," a " group
of people of good taste, good manners, reading
the best books, interpreting the best music,
interested in themes world-wide, the peers of
any people in the world," is it credible, with the
instinct of self-preservation which there is in
humanity, and choice things being so naturally
attractive as they undoubtedly are, — is it credi-

ble, that all this excellent leaven should produce so little result, that these groups should
remain so impotent and isolated, that their
environment, in a country where our poverty is
unknown, should be "a world in which not one
man in a hundred thousand has either the manners or cultivation of a gentleman, or changes
his shirt more than once a week, or eats with
a fork?" It is not credible; to me, at any
rate, it is not credible. And I feel more sure
than ever, that our Boston informant has told
us of groups where he ought to have told us of
individuals; and that many of his individuals,
even, have "hopped over," as he wittily says,
to Europe.

Mr. Lowell himself describes his own nation
as "the most common-schooled and the least
cultivated people in the world." They strike
foreigners in the same way. M. Renan says
that the "United States have created a considerable popular instruction without any serious higher instruction, and will long have to
expiate this fault by their intellectual medioc-
rity, their vulgarity of manners, their superfi-
cial spirit, their lack of general intelligence."
Another acute French critic speaks of a "hard
unintelligence" as characteristic of the people
of the United States — *la dure inintelligence*

des Américains du Nord. Smart they are, as
all the world knows ; but then smartness is un-
happily quite compatible with a " hard unintelligence." The Quinionian humour of Mr. Mark
Twain, so attractive to the Philistine of the
more gay and light type both here and in
America, another French critic fixes upon as
literature exactly expressing a people of this
type, and of no higher. " In spite of all its
primary education," he says, " America is still,
from an intellectual point of view, a very rude
and primitive soil, only to be cultivated by
violent methods. These childish and half-sav-
age minds are not moved except by very ele-
mentary narratives composed without art, in
which burlesque and melodrama, vulgarity and
eccentricity, are combined in strong doses."
It may be said that Frenchmen, the present
generation of Frenchmen at any rate, themselves take seriously, as of the family of
Shakespeare, Molière, and Goethe, an author
half genius, half charlatan, like M. Victor Hugo.
They do so ; but still they may judge, soundly
and correctly enough, another nation's false
literature which does not appeal to their weak-
nesses. I am not blaming America for falling
a victim to Quinion, or to Murdstone either.
We fall a victim to Murdstone and Quinion our

selves, as I very well know, and the Americans are just the same people that we are. But I want to deliver England from Murdstone and Quinion, and I look round me for help in the good work. And when the Boston newspaper told me of the elegant and simple social order, and the group of people in every town of the Union with good taste and good manners, reading the best books and interpreting the best music, I thought at first that I had surely found what I wanted, and that I should be able to invade the English realm of Murdstone and Quinion with the support of an overpowering body of allies from America. But now it seems doubtful whether America is not suffering from the predominance of Murdstone and Quinion herself — of Quinion at any rate.

Yes, and of Murdstone too. Miss Bird, the best of travellers, and with the skill to relate her travels delightfully, met the rudimentary American type of Murdstone not far from Denver, and has described him for us. Denver — I hear some one say scornfully — Denver! A new territory, the outskirts of civilization, the Rocky Mountains! But I prefer to follow a course which would, I know, deliver me over a prey into the Americans' hands, if I were really holding a controversy with them and attacking

their civilization. I am not holding a controversy with them. I am not attacking their
civilization. I am much disquieted about the
state of our own. But I am holding a friendly
conversation with American lovers of the humane life, who offer me hopes of improving
British civilization by the example of a great
force of true civilization, of elegant and simple
social order, developed in the northern, middle,
and southwestern states of the Union. I am
not going to pick holes in the civilization of
those well-established States. But in a new
territory, on the outskirts of the Union, I take
an example of a spirit which we know well
enough in the old country, and which has done
much harm to our civilization; and I ask my
American friends how much way this spirit —
since on their borders, at any rate, they seem
to have it — has made and is even now making
amongst themselves; whether they feel sure of
getting it under control, and that the elegant
and simple social order in the older states will
be too strong for it; or whether, on the other
hand, it may be too strong for the elegant and
simple social order.

Miss Bird then describes the Chalmers family, a family with which, on her journey from
Denver to the Rocky Mountains, she lodged for

some time.   Miss Bird, as those who have read her books well know, is not a lackadaisical person, or in any way a fine lady ; she can ride, catch, and saddle a horse, "make herself agreeable," wash up plates, improvise lamps, teach knitting.   But —

Oh (she says), what a hard, narrow life it is with which I am now in contact !   A narrow and unattractive religion, which I believe still to be genuine, and an intense but narrow patriotism, are the only higher influences. Chalmers came from Illinois nine years ago.   He is slightly intelligent, very opinionated, and wishes to be thought well-informed, which he is not.   He belongs to the strictest sect of Reformed Presbyterians ; his great boast is that his ancestors were Scottish Covenanters. He considers himself a profound theologian, and by the pine logs at night discourses to me on the mysteries of the eternal counsels and the divine decrees.   Colorado, with its progress and its future, is also a constant theme. He hates England with a bitter personal hatred.   He trusts to live to see the downfall of the British monarchy and the disintegration of the empire.   He is very fond of talking, and asks me a great deal about my travels, but if I speak favorably of the climate or resources of any other country, he regards it as a slur on Colorado.

Mrs. Chalmers looks like one of the English poor women of our childhood — lean, clean, toothless, and speaks, like some of them, in a piping, discontented voice, which seems to convey a personal reproach.   She is never idle for one moment, is severe and hard, and despises everything but work.   She always speaks of me as *this* or *that woman.*   The family consists of a grown-up son,

a shiftless, melancholy-looking youth, who possibly pines
for a wider life ; a girl of sixteen, a sour, repellant-looking
creature, with as much manners as a pig ; and three
hard, unchildlike younger children. By the whole family
all courtesy and gentleness of act or speech seem regarded
as *works of the flesh*, if not of *the devil*. They knock
over all one's things without apologizing or picking them
up, and when I thank them for anything they look grimly
amazed. I wish I could show them "a more excellent
way." This hard greed, and the exclusive pursuit of
gain, with the indifference to all which does not aid in its
acquisition, are eating up family love and life throughout
the West. I write this reluctantly, and after a total experience of nearly two years in the United States. Mrs.
Chalmers is cleanly in her person and dress, and the food,
though poor, is clean. Work, work, work, is their day
and their life. They are thoroughly uncongenial. There
is a married daughter across the river, just the same hard,
loveless, moral, hard-working being as her mother. Each
morning, soon after seven, when I have swept the cabin,
the family come in for "worship." Chalmers wails a
psalm to the most doleful of dismal tunes ; they read a
chapter round, and he prays. Sunday was a dreadful day.
The family kept the commandment literally, and did no
work. Worship was conducted twice, and was rather
longer than usual. The man attempted to read a well-
worn copy of *Boston's Fourfold State*, but shortly fell
asleep, and they only woke up for their meals. It was an
awful day, and seemed as if it would never come to an
end. You will now have some idea of my surroundings.
It is a moral, hard, unloving, unlovely, unrelieved, un-
beautified, grinding life. These people live in a discom-
fort and lack of ease and refinement which seem only
possible to people of British stock.

What is this but the hideousness, the immense *ennui*, of the life on which we have touched so often, the life of our serious British Philistine, our Murdstone ; that life with its defective type of religion, its narrow range of intellect and knowledge, its stunted sense of beauty, its low standard of manners ? Only it is this life at its simplest, rudimentary stage.

I have purposely taken the picture of it from a region outside the settled states of the Union, that it might be evident I was not meaning to describe American civilization, and that Americans might at once be able to say, with perfect truth, that American civilization is something totally different. And if, to match this picture of our Murdstone in other lands and other cir- cumstances, we are to have — as, for the sake of clearness in our impressions, we ought to have — a picture of our Quinion too, under like conditions, let us take it, not from America at all, but from our own Australian colonies. The special correspondent of the *Bathurst Sentinel* criticises an Italian singer who, at the Sydney Theatre, plays the Count in the *Somnambula ;* and here is the criticism : " Barring his stom- ach, he is the finest-looking artist I have seen on the stage for years ; and if he don't slide into the affections or break the gizzards of half our Sydney girls, it's a pretty certain sign there's a scarcity of balm in Gilead." This is not Mark Twain, not an American humorist at all; it is the *Bathurst Sentinel.*

So I have gone to the Rocky Mountains for the New World Murdstone, and to Australia for the New World Quinion. I have not assailed in the least the civilization of America in those northern, middle, and southwestern states, to which Americans have a right to refer us when we seek to know their civilization, and to which they, in fact, do refer us. What I wish to say is, and I by no means even put it in the form of an assertion — I put it in the form of a question only, a question to my friends in America who are believers in equality and lovers of the humane life as I also am, and who ask me why I do not illustrate my praise of equality by reference to the humane life of America — what I wish to say is: How much does the influence of these two elements, natural products of our race, Murdstone and Quinion, the bitter, serious Philistine and the rowdy Philistine, enter into American life and lower it? I will not pronounce on the matter myself; I have not the requisite knowledge. But all that we hear from America — hear from Americans themselves — points, so far as I can see, to a great presence

and power of these middle-class misgrowths
there as here. We have not succeeded in
counteracting them here, and while our statesmen and leaders proceed as they do now, and
Lord Frederick Cavendish congratulates the
middle class on its energy and self-reliance in
doing without public schools, and Lord Salisbury summons the middle class to a great and
final stand on behalf of supernaturalism, we
never shall succeed in counteracting them. We
are told, however, of groups of children of light
in every town of America, and an elegant social
order prevailing there, which make one, at first,
very envious. But soon one begins to think, I
say, that surely there must be some mistake.
The complaints one hears of the state of public
life in America, of the increasing impossibility
and intolerableness of it to self-respecting men,
of the "corruption and feebleness," of the bla-
tant violence and exaggeration of language, the
profligacy of clap-trap — the complaints we hear
from America of all this, and then such an
exhibition as we had in the Guiteau trial the
other day, lead one to think that Murdstone
and Quinion, those misgrowths of the English
middle-class spirit, must be even more rampant
in the United States than they are here. Mr.
Lowell himself writes, in that very same essay

in which he is somewhat sharp upon foreigners,
he writes of the sad experience in America of
"government by declamation." And this very
week, as if to illustrate his words, we have the
American newspapers raising "a loud and per-
emptory voice" against the "gross outrage on
America, insulted in the persons of Americans
imprisoned in British dungeons"; we have them
crying: "The people demand their release, and
they must be released; woe to the public men
or the party that stand in the way of this act of
justice!" We have them turning upon Mr.
Lowell himself in such style as the following:
"This Lowell is a fraud, and a disgrace to the
American nation; Minister Lowell has scoffed
at his own country, and disowned everything in
its history and institutions that makes it free
and great."

I should say, for my part, though I have not,
I fully own, the means for judging accurately,
that all this points to an American development
of our Murdstone and Quinion, the bitter Philistine and the rowdy Philistine, exhibiting
themselves in conjunction, exhibiting themselves
with great luxuriance and with very little check.
As I write from Grub Street, I will add that, to
my mind, the condition of the copyright question between us and America appears to point

to just the same thing. The American refusal
of copyright to us poor English souls is just
the proceeding which would naturally commend
itself to Murdstone and Quinion ; and the way
in which Mr. Conant justifies and applauds the
proceeding, and continues to justify and applaud
it, in disregard of all that one may say, and
boldly turns the tables upon England, is just the
way in which Murdstone and Quinion, after re-
gulating copyright in the American fashion,
would wish and expect to be backed up. In
Mr. Conant they have a treasure : *illi robur et
æs triplex,* indeed. And no doubt a few Americans, highly civilized individuals, "hopping
backwards and forwards over the Atlantic,"
much disapprove of these words and works of
Mr. Conant and his constituents. But can there
be constant groups of children of light, joined
in an elegant order, everywhere throughout the
Union ? for, if there were, would not their sense
of equity, and their sense of delicacy, and even
their sense of the ridiculous, be too strong, even
in this very matter of copyright, for Mr. Conant
and his constituents ?

But on the creation and propagation of such
groups the civilized life of America depends for
its future, as the civilized life of our own country, too, depends for its future upon the same

thing ; — so much is certain.   And if America
succeeds in creating and installing hers, before
we succeed in creating and installing ours, then
they will send over help to us from America,
and will powerfully influence us for our good.
Let us see, then, how we both of us stand at
the present moment, and what advantages the
one of us has which are wanting to the other.
We in England have liberty and industry and
the sense for conduct, and a splendid aristocracy
which feels the need for beauty and manners,
and a unique class, as Mr. Charles Sumner
pointed out, of gentlemen, not of the landed
class or of the nobility, but cultivated and re-
fined.   America has not our splendid aristocracy,
but then this splendid aristocracy is materialized, and for helping the sense for beauty, or
the sense for social life and manners, in the nation at large, it does nothing or next to nothing.
So we must not hastily pronounce, with Mr.
Hussey Vivian, that American civilization suffers by its absence.   Indeed they are themselves
developing, it is said, a class of very rich people
quite sufficiently materialized.   America has
not our large and unique class of gentlemen ;
something of it they have, of course, but it is
not by any manner of means on the same scale
there as here.   Acting by itself, and untram

melled, our English class of gentlemen has
eminent merits ; our rule in India, of which we
may well be proud, is in great measure its work.
But in presence of a great force of Barbarian
power, as in this country, or in presence of a
great force of Philistinism, our class of gentlemen, as we know, has not much faith and ardor, is somewhat bounded and ineffective, is
not much of a civilized force for the nation at
large ; not much more, perhaps, than the few
" rather civilized individuals " in America, who,
according to our Boston informant, go " hopping
backwards and forwards over the Atlantic."
Perhaps America, with her needs, has no very
great loss in not having our special class of
gentlemen.   Without this class, and without the
pressure and false ideal of our Barbarians, the
Americans have, like ourselves, the sense for
conduct and religion ; they have industry, and
they have liberty ; they have, too, over and
above what we have, they have an excellent
thing — equality.   But we have seen reason for
thinking, that as we in England, with our aristocracy, gentlemen, liberty, industry, religion,
and sense for conduct, have the civilization of
the most important part of our people, the immense middle class, impaired by a defective type
of religion, a narrow range of intellect and

knowledge, a stunted sense of beauty, a low
standard of manners ; so in America, too, where
this class is yet more important and all-pervad-
ing than it is here, civilization suffers in the like
way.   With a people of our stock it could not,
indeed, well be otherwise, so long as this people
can be truly described as "the most common-
schooled and least cultivated people in the
world."

The real cultivation of the people of the
United States, as of the English middle class,
has been in and by its religion, its "one thing
needful."   But the insufficiency of this religion
is now every day becoming more manifest.   It
deals, indeed, with personages and words which
have an indestructible and inexhaustible truth
and salutariness ; but it is rooted and grounded
in preternaturalism, it can receive those personages and those words only on conditions of preternaturalism, and a religion of preternaturalism
is doomed — whether with or without the battle
of Armageddon for which Lord Salisbury is preparing — to inevitable dissolution.   *Fidelity to*
conscience ! cries the popular Protestanism of
Great Britain and America, and thinks that it
has said enough.   But the modern analysis re-
lentlessly scrutinizes this conscience, and com-
pels it to give an account of itself.   What sort

of a conscience? a true conscience or a false
one? "Conscience is the most changing of
rules; conscience is presumptuous in the strong,
timid in the weak and unhappy, wavering in the
undecided; obedient organ of the sentiment
which sways us and of the opinions which govern us; more misleading than reason and nature." So says one of the noblest and purest of
moralists, Vauvenargues; and terrible as it may
be to the popular Protestanism of England and
of America to hear it, Vauvenargues thus describes with perfect truth that conscience to
which popular Protestanism appeals as its supposed unshakable ground of reliance.

And now, having up to this point neglected
all the arts of the controversialist, having merely
made inquiries of my American friends as to
the real state of their civilization, inquiries
which they are free to answer in their own
favor if they like, I am going to leave the advantage with them to the end. They kindly offered me the example of their civilization as a
help to mend ours; and I, not with any vain
Anglicism, for I own our insular civilization to
be very unsatisfactory, but from a desire to get
at the truth and not to deceive myself with
hopes of help from a quarter where at present
there is none to be found, have inquired whether

the Americans really think, on looking into the matter, that their civilization is much more satisfactory than ours. And in case they should come to the conclusion, after due thought, that neither the one civilization nor the other is in a satisfactory state, let me end by propounding a remedy which really it is heroic in me to propound, for people are bored to death, they say, by me with it, and every time I mention it I make new enemies and diminish the small number of friends that I have now. Still, I cannot help asking whether the defects of American civilization, if it is defective, may not probably be connected with the American people's being, as Mr. Lowell says, " the most common-schooled and the least cultivated people in the world." A higher, larger cultivation, a finer lucidity, is what is needed. The friends of civilization, instead of hopping backwards and forwards over the Atlantic, should stay at home a while, and do their best to make the administration, the tribunals, the theatre, the arts, in each state, to make them become visible ideals to raise, purge, and ennoble the public sentiment. Though they may be few in number, the friends of civilization will find, probably, that by a serious apostolate of this kind they can accomplish a good deal. But the really fruitful reform to be looked

for in America, so far as I can judge, is the very
same reform which is so urgently required here
— a reform of secondary instruction. The primary and common schools of America we all
know; their praise is in every one's mouth.
About superior or University instruction one
need not be uneasy, it excites so much ambition,
is so much in view, and is required by comparatively so small a number. An institution like
Harvard is probably all that one could desire.
But really good secondary schools, to form a due
proportion of the youth of America from the
age of twelve to the age of eighteen, and then
every year to throw a supply of them, thus
formed, into circulation — this is what America,
I believe, wants, as we also want it, and what
she possesses no more than we do. I know she
has higher schools, I know their programme :
Latin, Greek, German, French, Surveying,
Chemistry, Astrology, Natural History, Mental
Philosophy, Constitution, Bookkeeping, Trigono-
metry, etc. Alas, to quote Vauvenargues again:
" *On ne corrigera jamais les hommes d'apprendre
des choses inutiles !* " But good secondary
schools, not with the programme of our classical and commercial academies, but with a serious programme — a programme really suited to
the wants and capacities of those who are to be

trained — this, I repeat, is what American civilization in my belief most requires, as it is what our civilization, too, at present most requires. The special present defects of both American civilization and ours are the kind of defects for which this is a natural remedy.   I commend it to the attention of my friendly Boston critic in America ; and some months hence, perhaps, when Mr. Barnum begins to require less space for his chronicles of Jumbo, my critic will tell me what he thinks of it.

A WORD MORE ABOUT AMERICA.

III.

A WORD MORE ABOUT AMERICA.

WHEN I was at Chicago last year, I was asked whether Lord Coleridge would not write a book about America. I ventured to answer confidently for him that he would do nothing of the kind. Not at Chicago only, but almost wherever I went, I was asked whether I myself did not intend to write a book about America. For oneself one can answer yet more confidently than for one's friends, and I always replied that most assuredly I had no such intention. To write a book about America, on the strength of having made merely such a tour there as mine was, and with no fuller equipment of preparatory studies and of local observations than I possess, would seem to me an impertinence.

It is now a long while since I read M. de Tocqueville's famous work on Democracy in America. I have the highest respect for M. de Tocqueville; but my remembrance of his book is that it deals too much in abstractions for my taste, and that it is written, moreover, in a style which many French writers adopt, but which I find trying — a style cut into short paragraphs and wearing an air of rigorous scientific deduction without the reality. Very likely, however, I do M. de Tocqueville injustice. My debility in high speculation is well known, and I mean to attempt his book on Democracy again when I have seen America once more, and when years may have brought to me, perhaps, more of the philosophic mind. Meanwhile, however, it will be evident how serious a matter I think it to write a worthy book about the United States, when I am not entirely satisfied with even M. de Tocqueville's.

But before I went to America, and when I had no expectation of ever going there, I published, under the title of "A Word about America," not indeed a book, but a few modest remarks on what I thought civilization in the United States might probably be like. I had before me a Boston newspaper article, which said that if I ever visited America I should find there such and such things; and taking this article for my text I observed that from all I had read and all I could judge I should for my part expect to find there rather such and such other things, which I mentioned. I said that of aristocracy, as we know it here, I should expect to find, of course, in the United States the total absence ; that our lower class I should expect to find absent in a great degree, while my old familiar friend, the middle class, I should expect to find in full possession of the land. And then betaking myself to those playful phrases which a little relieve, perhaps, the tedium of grave disquisitions of this sort, I said that I imagined one would just have in America our Philistines, with our aristocracy quite left out, and our populace very nearly.

An acute and singularly candid American, whose name I will on no account betray to his countrymen, read these observations of mine, and he made a remark upon them to me which struck me a good deal. Yes, he said, you are right, and your supposition is just. In general, what you would find over there would be the Philistines, as you call them, without your aristocracy and without your populace. Only this, too, I say at the same time : you would find over there something besides, something more, something which you do not bring out, which you cannot know and bring out, perhaps, without actually visiting the United States, but which you would recognize if you saw it.

My friend was a true prophet. When I saw

the United States I recognized that the general
account which I had hazarded of them was,
indeed, not erroneous, but that it required to
have something added to supplement it.   I
should not like either my friends in America or
my countrymen here at home to think that my
" Word about America" gave my full and final
thoughts respecting the people of the United
States.   The new and modifying impressions
brought by experience I shall communicate, as
I did my original expectations, with all good
faith, and as simply and plainly as possible.
Perhaps when I have yet again visited America, have seen the great West, and have had a
second reading of M. de Tocqueville's classical
work on Democracy, my mind may be enlarged
and my present impressions still further modi-
fied by new ideas.   If so, I promise to make my
confession duly ; not indeed to make it, even
then, in a book about America, but to make it
in a brief " Last Word " on that great subject
— a word, like its predecessors, of open-
hearted and free conversation with the readers
of this review.

I suppose I am not by nature disposed to
think so much as most people do of "institutions."   The Americans think and talk very

much of their "institutions;" I am by nature inclined to call all this sort of thing *machinery*, and to regard, rather, men and their characters. But the more I saw of America, the more I found myself led to treat "institutions" with increased respect. Until I went to the United States I had never seen a people with institutions which seemed expressly and thoroughly suited to it. I had not properly appreciated the benefits proceeding from this cause.

Sir Henry Maine, in an admirable essay which, though not signed, betrays him for its author by its rare and characteristic qualities of mind and style — Sir Henry Maine, in the *Quarterly Review*, adopts and often reiterates a phrase of M. Scherer, to the effect that "Democracy is only a form of government." He holds up to ridicule a sentence of Mr. Bancroft's History, in which the American democracy is told that its ascent to power "proceeded as uniformly and majestically as the laws of being, and was as certain as the decrees of eternity." Let us be willing to give Sir Henry Maine his way, and to allow no magnificent claim of this kind on behalf of the American democracy. Let us treat as not more solid the assertion in the Declaration of Independence, that "all men are created equal, and endowed

by their Creator with certain inalienable rights,
among them life, liberty, and the pursuit of
happiness." Let us concede that these natural
rights are a figment ; that chance and circumstance, as much as deliberate foresight and
design, have brought the United States into
their present condition; that, moreover, the
British rule which they threw off was not the
rule of oppressors and tyrants which declaimers
suppose, and that the merit of the Americans
was not that of oppressed men rising against
tyrants, but rather of sensible young people
getting rid of stupid and overweening guardians
who misunderstood and mismanaged them.

All this let us concede, if we will ; but in
conceding it let us not lose sight of the really
important point, which is this : that their institutions do in fact suit the people of the United
States so well, and that from this suitableness
they do derive so much actual benefit. As one
watches the play of their institutions, the image
suggests itself to one's mind of a man in a suit
of clothes which fits him to perfection, leaving
all his movements unimpeded and easy. It is
loose where it ought to be loose, and it sits
close where its sitting close is an advantage.
The central government of the United States
keeps in its own hands the functions which, if

the nation is to have real unity, ought to be kept there; those functions it takes to itself, and no others. The state governments and the municipal governments provide people with the fullest liberty of managing their own affairs, and afford, besides, a constant and invaluable school of practical experience. This wonderful suit of clothes, again (to recur to our image), is found also to adapt itself naturally to the wearer's growth, and to admit of all enlargements as they successively arise. I speak of the state of things since the suppression of slavery, — of the state of things which meets a spectator's eye at the present time in America. There are points in which the institutions of the United States may call forth criticism. One observer may think that it would be well if the President's term of office were longer, if his ministers sate in Congress, or must possess the confidence of Congress. Another observer may say that the marriage laws for the whole nation ought to be fixed by Congress, and not to vary at the will of the legislatures of the several States. I myself was much struck with the inconvenience of not allowing a man to sit in Congress except for his own district; a man like Wendell Phillips was thus excluded, because Boston would not return him. It is as if

Mr. Bright could have no other constituency
open to him if Rochdale would not send him to
Parliament.   But all these are really questions
of *machinery* (to use my own term), and ought
not so to engage our attention as to prevent our
seeing that the capital fact as to the institutions
of the United States is this : their suitableness
to the American people, and their natural and
easy working.   If we are not to be allowed to
say, with Mr. Beecher, that this people has "a
genius for the organization of states," then at
all events we must admit that in its own organization it has enjoyed the most signal good
fortune.

Yes ; what is called in the jargon of the publicists, the political problem and the social
problem, the people of the United States does
appear to me to have solved, or Fortune has
solved it for them, with undeniable success.
Against invasion and conquest from without
they are impregnably strong.   As to domestic
concerns, the first thing to remember is, that
the people over there is at bottom the same
people as ourselves, — a people with a strong
sense for conduct.   But there is said to be
much corruption among their politicians, and in
the public service, in municipal administration,
and in the administration of justice.   Sir Lepel

Griffin would lead us to think that the administration of justice, in particular, is so thoroughly
corrupt, that a man with a lawsuit has only to
provide his lawyer with the necessary funds for
bribing the officials, and he can make sure of
winning his suit. The Americans themselves
use such strong language in describing the corruption prevalent amongst them, that they cannot be surprised if strangers believe them. For
myself, I had heard and read so much to the
discredit of American political life, how all the
best men kept aloof from it, and those who
gave themselves to it were unworthy, that I
ended by supposing that the thing must actually
be so, and the good Americans must be looked
for elsewhere than in politics. Then I had the
pleasure of dining with Mr. Bancroft in Washington ; and however he may, in Sir Henry
Maine's opinion, overlaud the pre-established
harmony of American democracy, he had at any
rate invited to meet me half a dozen politicians
whom in England we should pronounce to be
members of Parliament of the highest class, in
bearing, manners, tone of feeling, intelligence,
information. I discovered that in truth the
practice, so common in America, of calling a
politician "a thief" does not mean so very
much more than is meant in England when we

have heard Lord Beaconsfield called "a liar,"
and Mr. Gladstone, "a madman." It means,
that the speaker disagrees with the politician in
question, and dislikes him. Not that I assent,
on the other hand, to the thick-and-thin American patriots, who will tell you that there is no
more corruption in the politics and administration of the United States than in those of
England. I believe there *is* more, and that the
tone of both is lower there; and this from a
cause on which I shall have to touch hereafter.
But the corruption is exaggerated; it is not the
wide and deep disease it is often represented;
it is such that the good elements in the nation
may, and I believe will, perfectly work it off;
and even now the truth of what I have been
saying as to the suitableness and successful
working of American institutions is not really
in the least affected by it.

Furthermore, American society is not in
danger from revolution. Here, again, I do not
mean that the United States are exempt from
the operation of every one of the causes — such
a cause as the division between rich and poor,
for instance — which may lead to revolution.
But I mean that comparatively with the old
countries of Europe they are free from the danger of revolution; and I believe that the good

elements in them will make a way for them to
escape out of what they really have of this.
danger also, to escape in the future as well as,
now — the future for which some observer,
announce this danger as so certain and so for,
midable. Lord Macaulay predicted that the
United States must come in time to just the
same state of things which we witness in Eng;
land; that the cities would fill up and the land,
become occupied, and then, he said, the division
between rich and poor would establish itself or:
the same scale as with us, and be just as embar.
rassing. He forgot that the United States are
without what certainly fixes and accentuates the
division between rich and poor, — the distinc·
tion of classes. Not only have they not the
distinction between noble and bourgeois, be
tween aristocracy and middle class; they hav;
not even the distinction between bourgeois an,
peasant or artisan, between middle and lowe;
class. They have nothing to create it an;
compel their recognition of it. Their domesti;
service is done for them by Irish, Germans
Swedes, negroes. Outside domestic service.
within the range of conditions which an Amer
ican may, in fact, be called upon to traverse, he
passes easily from one sort of occupation to
another, from poverty to riches, and from riches

to poverty. No one of his possible occupations
appears degrading to him or makes him lose
caste; and poverty itself appears to him as
inconvenient and disagreeable rather than as
humiliating. When the immigrant from Europe
strikes root in his new home, he becomes as the
American.

It may be said that the Americans, when
they attained their independence, had not the
elements for a division into classes, and that
they deserve no praise for not having invented
one. But I am not now contending that they
deserve praise for their institutions, I am saying
how well their institutions work. Considering,
indeed, how rife are distinctions of rank and
class in the world, how prone men in general
are to adopt them, how much the Americans
themselves, beyond doubt, are capable of feeling their attraction, it shows, I think, at least
strong good sense in the Americans to have
forborne from all attempt to invent them at the
outset, and to have escaped or resisted any
fancy for inventing them since. But evidently
the United States constituted themselves, not
amid the circumstances of a feudal age, but in a
modern age; not under the conditions of an
epoch favorable to subordination, but under
those of an epoch of expansion. Their institu-

tions did but comply with the form and pressure
of the circumstances and conditions then present. A feudal age, an epoch of war, defence,
and concentration, needs centres of power and
property, and it reinforces property by joining
distinctions of rank and class with it. Property
becomes more honorable, more solid. And in
feudal ages this is well, for its changing hands
easily would be a source of weakness. But in
ages of expansion, where men are bent that
every one shall have his chance, the more
readily property changes hands the better.
The envy with which its holder is regarded
diminishes, society is safer. I think whatever
may be said of the worship of the almighty
dollar in America, it is indubitable that rich
men are regarded there with less envy and
hatred than rich men are in Europe. Why is
this? Because their condition is less fixed,
because government and legislation do not take
them more seriously than other people, make
grandees of them, aid them to found families
and endure. With us, the chief holders of
property are grandees already, and every rich
man aspires to become a grandee if possible.
And therefore an English country gentleman
regards himself as part of the system of nature;
government and legislation have invited him so

to do. If the price of wheat falls so low that his means of expenditure are greatly reduced, he tells you that if this lasts he cannot possibly go on as a country gentleman ; and every well-bred person amongst us looks sympathizing and shocked. An American would say, "Why should he?" The conservative newspapers are fond of giving us, as an argument for the game laws, the plea that without them a country gentleman could not be induced to live on his estate. An American would say, "What does it matter?" Perhaps to an English ear this will sound brutal ; but the point is that the American does not take his rich man so seriously as we do ours, does not make him into a grandee ; the thing, if proposed to him, would strike him as an absurdity. I suspect that Mr. Winans himself, the American millionaire who adds deer-forest to deer-forest, and will not suffer a cottier to keep a pet lamb, regards his own performance as a colossal stroke of American humor, illustrating the absurdities of the British system of property and privilege. Ask Mr. Winans if he would promote the introduction of the British game laws into the United States, and he would tell you with a merry laugh that the idea is ridiculous, and that these British follies are for home consumption.

"The example of France must not mislead us. There the institutions, an objector may say, are republican, and yet the division and hatred between rich and poor is intense. True ; but in France, though the institutions may be republican, the ideas and morals are not republican. In America not only are the institutions republican, but the ideas and morals are prevailingly republican also. They are those of a plain, decent middle class. The ideal of those who are the public instructors of the people is the ideal of such a class. In France the ideal of the mass of popular journalists and popular writers of fiction, who are now practically the public instructors there, is, if you could see their hearts, a Pompadour or du Barry *régime*, with themselves for the part of Faublas. With this ideal prevailing, this vision of the objects for which wealth is desirable, the possessors of wealth become hateful to the multitude which toils and endures, and society is undermined. This is one of the many inconveniences which the French have to suffer from that worship of the great goddess Lubricity to which they are at present vowed. Wealth excites the most savage enmity there, because it is conceived as a means for gratifying appetites of the most selfish and vile kind. But in America, Faublas

is no more the ideal than Coriolanus. Wealth
is no more conceived as the minister to the
pleasures of a class of rakes, than as the minister to the magnificence of a class of nobles. It
is conceived as a thing which almost any
American may attain, and which almost every
American will use respectably. Its possession,
therefore, does not inspire hatred, and so I
return to the thesis with which I started —
America is not in danger of revolution. The
division between rich and poor is alleged to us
as a cause of revolution which presently, if not
now, must operate there, as elsewhere; and yet
we see that this cause has not there, in truth,
the characters to which we are elsewhere accustomed.

A people homogeneous, a people which had
to constitute itself in a modern age, an epoch of
expansion, and which has given to itself institutions entirely fitted for such an age and epoch,
and which suit it perfectly — a people not in
danger of war from without, not in danger of
revolution from within — such is the people of
the United States. The political and social
problem, then, we must surely allow that they
solve successfully. There remains, I know, the
human problem also; the solution of that too
has to be considered; but I shall come to that

hereafter. My point at present is, that politically and socially the United States are a
community living in a natural condition, and
conscious of living in a natural condition. And
being in this healthy case, and having this
healthy consciousness, the community there
uses its understanding with the soundness of
health ; it in general sees its political and social
concerns straight, and sees them clear. So
that when Sir Henry Maine and M. Scherer
tells us that democracy is "merely a form of
government," we may observe to them that it
is in the United States a form of government
in which the community feels itself in a natural
condition and at ease ; in which, consequently,
it sees things straight and sees them clear.

More than half one's interest in watching the
English people of the United States comes, of
course, from the bearing of what one finds there
upon things at home, amongst us English
people ourselves in these islands. I have
frankly recorded what struck me and came as
most new to me in the condition of the English
race in the United States, I had said beforehand, indeed, that I supposed the American
Philistine was a livelier sort of Philistine than
ours, because he had not that pressure of the
Barbarians to stunt and distort him which be-

falls his English brother here. But I did not
foresee how far his superior liveliness and natu-
ralness of condition, in the absence of that
pressure, would carry the American Philistine.
I still use my old name *Philistine*, because it
does in fact seem to me as yet to suit the bulk
of the community over there, as it suits the
strong central body of the community here.
But in my mouth the name is hardly a reproach.
so clearly do I see the Philistine's necessity, so
willingly I own his merits, so much I find of
him in myself. The American Philistine, however, is certainly far more different from his
English brother than I had beforehand supposed. And on that difference we English of
the old country may with great profit turn our
regards for a while, and I am now going to speak
of it.

Surely, if there is one thing more than another
which all the world is saying of our community
at present, and of which the truth cannot well
be disputed, it is this : that we act like people
who do not think straight and see clear. I
know that the Liberal newspapers used to be
fond of saying that what characterized our
middle class was its "clear, manly intelligence,
penetrating through sophisms, ignoring com-
monplaces, and giving to conventional illu-

sions their true value." Many years ago I took
alarm at seeing the *Daily News* and the *Morning Star*, like Zedekiah the son of Chenaanah,
thus making horns of iron for the middle class
and bidding it "Go up and prosper!" and my
first efforts as a writer on public matters were
prompted by a desire to utter, like Micaiah, the
son of Imlah, my protest against these misleading assurances of the false prophets. And
though often and often smitten on the cheek,
just as Micaiah was, still I persevered; and at
the Royal Institution I said how we seemed to
flounder and to beat the air, and at Liverpool I
singled out as our chief want the want of lucidity. But now everybody is really saying of us
the same thing: that we fumble because we
cannot make up our mind, and that we cannot
make up our mind because we do not know
what to be after. If our foreign policy is not
that of "the British Philistine, with his likes
and dislikes, his effusion and confusion, his hot
and cold fits, his want of dignity and of the
steadfastness which comes from dignity, his
want of ideas, and of the steadfastness which
comes from ideas," then all the world at the
present time is, it must be owned, very much
mistaken.

Let us not, therefore, speak of foreign affairs;

it is needless, because the thing I wish to show
is so manifest there to everybody.   But we will
consider matters at home.   Let us take the
present state of the House of Commons.   Can
anything be more confused, more unnatural?
That assembly has got into a condition utterly
embarrassed, and seems impotent to bring itself
right.   The members of the House themselves
may find entertainment in the personal inci-
dents which such a state of confusion is sure
to bring forth abundantly, and excitement in
the opportunities thus often afforded for the
display of Mr. Gladstone's wonderful powers.
But to any judicious Englishman outside the
House the spectacle is simply an afflicting and
humiliating one ; the sense aroused by it is not
a sense of delight at Mr. Gladstone's tireless
powers, it is rather a sense of disgust at their
having to be so exercised.   Every day the
House of Commons does not sit, judicious
people feel relief; every day that it sits, they
are oppressed with apprehension.   Instead of
being an edifying influence, as such an assembly ought to be, the House of Commons is at
present an influence which does harm ; it sets
an example which rebukes and corrects none of
the nation's faults, but rather encourages them.
The best thing to be done at present, perhaps,

is to avert one's eye from the House of Commons as much as possible ; if one keeps on constantly watching it welter in its baneful confusion, one is likely to fall into the fulminating style of the wrathful Hebrew prophets, and to call it "an astonishment, a hissing, and a curse."

Well, then, our greatest institution, the House of Commons, we cannot say is at present working, like the American institutions, easily and successfully. Suppose we now pass to Ireland. I will not ask if our institutions work easily and successfully in Ireland ; to ask such a question would be too bitter, too cruel a mockery. Those hateful cases which have been tried in the Dublin Courts this last year suggest the dark and ill-omened word which applies to the whole state of Ireland — *anti-natural. Anti-natural, anti-nature* ; that is the word which rises irresistibly in the mind as I survey Ireland. Everything is unnatural there: the proceedings of the English who rule, the proceedings of the Irish who resist. But it is with the working of our English institutions there that I am now concerned. It is unnatural that Ireland should be governed by Lord Spencer and Mr. Campbell Bannerman ; as unnatural as for Scotland to be governed by Lord

Cranbrook and Mr. Heally. It is unnatural
that Ireland should be governed under the
Crimes Act. But there is necessity, replies
the Government. Well, then, if there is such
an evil necessity, it is unnatural that the Irish
newspapers should be free to write as they
write and the Irish members to speak as they
speak, — free to inflame and further to exasper-
ate a seditious people's mind, and to promote
the continuance of the evil necessity. A necessity for the Crimes Act is a necessity for absolute government. By our patchwork proceedings
we set up, indeed, a make-believe of Ireland's
being constitutionally governed. But it is not
constitutionally governed ; nobody supposes it
to be constitutionally governed, except, perhaps,
that born swallower of all clap-trap, the British
Philistine. The Irish themselves, the all-im-
portant personages in this case, are not taken
in ; our make-believe does not produce in them
the very least gratitude, the very least soften-
ing. At the same time, it adds an hundredfold
to the difficulties of an absolute government.

The working of our institutions being thus
awry, is the working of our thoughts upon them
more smooth and natural ? I imagine to myself
an American, his own institutions and his habits
of thought being such as we have seen, listen-

ing to us as we talk politics and discuss the
strained state of things over there. " Certainly
these men have considerable difficulties," he
would say; "but they never look at them
straight, they do not think straight." Who
does not admire the fine qualities of Lord
Spencer? — and I, for my part, am quite ready
to admit that he may require for a given period
not only the present Crimes Act, but even yet
more stringent powers of repression. *For a
given period*, yes! — but afterwards? Has
Lord Spencer any clear vision of the great,
the profound changes still to be wrought before a staple and prosperous society can arise
in Ireland? Has he even any ideal for the future there, beyond that of a time when he can
go to visit Lord Kenmare, or any other great
landlord who is his friend, and find all the
tenants punctually paying their rents, prosperous and deferential, and society in Ireland set-
tling quietly down again upon the old basis?
And he might as well hope to see Strongbow
come to life again! Which of us does not
esteem and like Mr. Trevelyan, and rejoice in
the high promise of his career? And how all
his friends applauded when he turned upon the
exasperating and insulting Irish members, and
told them that he was " an English gentle-

man!" Yet, if one thinks of it, Mr. Trevelyan was thus telling the Irish members simply that he was just that which Ireland does not want, and which can do her no good. England, to be sure, has given Ireland plenty of her worst, but she has also given her not scantily of her best. Ireland has had no insufficient supply of the English gentleman, with his honesty, personal courage, high bearing, good intentions, and limited vision; what she wants is statesmen with just the qualities which the typical English gentleman has not — flexibility, openness of mind, a free and large view of things.

Everywhere we shall find in our thinking, a sort of warp inclining it aside of the real mark, and thus depriving it of value. The common run of peers who write to the *Times* about Reform of the House of Lords one would not much expect, perhaps, to " understand the signs of this time." But even the Duke of Argyle, delivering his mind about the land question in Scotland, is like one seeing, thinking, and speaking in some other planet than ours. A man of even Mr. John Morley's gifts is provoked with the House of Lords, and straightway he declares himself against the existence of a Second Chamber at all; although — if there be such a thing as demonstration in politics — the working of the American Senate demonstrates a well-composed Second Chamber to be the very need and safeguard of a modern democracy. What a singular twist, again, in a man of Mr. Frederic Harrison's intellectual power, not, perhaps, to have in the exuberance of youthful energy weighted himself for the race of life by taking up a grotesque old French pedant upon his shoulders, but to have insisted, in middle age, in taking up the Protestant Dissenters too ; and now, when he is becoming elderly, it seems as if nothing would serve him but he must add the Peace Society to his load ! How perverse, yet again, in Mr. Herbert Spencer, at the very moment when past neglects and present needs are driving men to co-operation, to making the community act for the public good in its collective and corporate character of *the State*, how perverse to seize this occasion for promulgating the extremest doctrine of individualism ; and not only to drag this dead horse along the public road himself, but to induce Mr. Auberon Herbert to devote his days to flogging it !

We think thus unaccountably because we are living in an unnatural and strained state. We are like people whose vision is deranged by their looking through a turbid and distorting .

atmosphere, or whose movements are warped by the cramping of some unnatural constraint. Let us just ask ourselves, looking at the thing as people simply desirous of finding the truth, how men who saw and thought straight would proceed, how an American, for instance, — whose seeing and thinking has, I have said, if not in all matters, yet commonly in political and social concerns, this quality of straightness, — how an American would proceed in the three confusions which I have given as instances of the many confusions now embarrassing us : the confusion of our foreign affairs, the confusion of the House of Commons, the confusion of Ireland.   And then, when we have discovered the kind of proceeding natural in these cases, let us ask ourselves, with the same sincerity, what is the cause of that warp of mind hindering most of us from seeing straight in them, and also where is our remedy.

The Angra Pequeña business has lately called forth from all sides many and harsh animadversions upon Lord Granville, who is charged with the direction of our foreign affairs.   I shall not swell the chorus of complainers. Nothing has happened but what was to be expected.   Long ago I remarked that it is not Lord Granville himself who determines our

foreign policy and shapes the declarations of
Government concerning it, but a power behind
Lord Granville.   He and his colleagues would
call it the power of public opinion.   It is really
the opinion of that great ruling class amongst
us on which Liberal Governments have hitherto
had to depend for support, — the Philistines or
middle class.   It is not, I repeat, with Lord
Granville in his natural state and force that a
foreign Government has to deal ; it is with
Lord Granville waiting in devout expectation to
see how the cat will jump, — and that cat the
British Philistine! When Prince Bismarck
deals with Lord Granville, he finds that he is
not dealing mind to mind with an intelligent
equal, but that he is dealing with a tumult of
likes and dislikes, hopes and fears, stock-job-
bing intrigues, missionary interests, quidnuncs,
newspapers ; — dealing, in short, with *ignorance*
behind his intelligent equal.   Yet ignorant as
our Philistine middle class may be, its volitions
on foreign affairs would have more intelligi-
bility and consistency if uttered through a
spokesman of their own class.   Coming through
a nobleman like Lord Granville, who has neither
the thoughts, habits, nor ideals of the middle
class, and yet wishes to act as proctor for it,
they have every disadvantage.   He cannot even

do justice to the Philistine mind, such as it is,
for which he is spokesman ; he apprehends it
uncertainly and expounds it ineffectively.   And
so with the house and lineage of Murdstone
thundering at him (and these, again, through
Lord Derby as their interpreter) from the Cape,
and the inexorable Prince Bismarck thundering
at him from Berlin, the thing naturally ends by
Lord Granville at last wringing his adroit hands
and ejaculating disconsolately :   " It is a misun-
derstanding altogether ! "   Even yet more to
be pitied, perhaps, was the hard case of Lord
Kimberly after the Majuba Hill disaster.   Who
can ever forget him, poor man, studying the
faces of the representatives of the dissenting
interest and exclaiming :   " A sudden thought
strikes me !   May we not be incurring the sin
of blood-guiltiness ? "   To this has come the
tradition of Lord Somers, the Whig oligarchy
of 1688, and all Lord Macaulay's Pantheon.

I said that a source of strength to America,
in political and social concerns, was the homogeneous character of American society.   An
American statesman speaks with more effect
the mind of his fellow-citizens from his being in
sympathy with it, understanding and sharing it.
Certainly, one must admit that if, in our country of classes, the Philistine middle class is

really the inspirer of our foreign policy, that policy would at least be expounded more forcibly if it had a Philistine for its spokesman. Yet I think the true moral to be drawn is rather, perhaps, this: that our foreign policy would be improved if our whole society were homogeneous.

As to the confusion in the House of Commons, what, apart from defective rules of procedure, are its causes? First and foremost, no doubt, the temper and action of the Irish members. But putting this cause of confusion out of view for a moment, every one can see that the House of Commons is far too large, and that it undertakes a quantity of business which belongs more properly to local assemblies. The confusion from these causes is one which is constantly increasing, because, as the country becomes fuller and more awakened, business multiplies, and more and more members of the House are inclined to take part in it. Is not the cure for this found in a course like that followed in America, in having a much less numerous House of Commons, and in making over a large part of its business to local assemblies, elected, as the House of Commons itself will henceforth be elected, by household suffrage? I have often said that we seem to me to need at present, in England, three things in especial : more equality, education for the middle classes, and a thorough municipal system. A system of local assemblies is but the natural complement of a thorough municipal system. Wholes neither too large nor too small, not necessarily of equal population by any means, but with characters rendering them in themselves fairly homogeneous and coherent, are the fit units for choosing these local assemblies. Such units occur immediately to one's mind in the provinces of Ireland, the Highlands and Lowlands of Scotland, Wales, north and south, groups of English counties such as present themselves in the circuits of the judges or under the names of East Anglia or the Midlands. No one will suppose me guilty of the pedantry of here laying out definitive districts ; I do but indicate such units as may enable the reader to conceive the kind of basis required for the local assemblies of which I am speaking. The business of these districts would be more advantageously done in assemblies of the kind ; they would form a useful school for the increasing number of aspirants to public life, and the House of Commons would be relieved.

The strain in Ireland would be relieved too, and by natural and safe means. Irishmen are

to be found, who, in desperation at the present
state of their country, cry out for making Ireland independent and separate, with a national
Parliament in Dublin, with her own foreign
office and diplomacy, her own army and navy,
her own tariff, coinage, and currency. This is
manifestly impracticable. But here again let
us look at what is done by people who in politics think straight and see clear ; let us observe
what is done in the United States. The Government at Washington reserves matters of imperial concern, matters such as those just enu-
merated, which cannot be relinquished without
relinquishing the unity of the empire. Neither
does it allow one great South to be constituted,
or one great West, with a Southern Parliament,
or a Western. Provinces that are too large are
broken up, as Virginia has been broken up.
But the several States are nevertheless real and
important wholes, each with its own legislature ; and to each the control, within its own
borders, of all except imperial concerns is freely
committed. The United States Government
intervenes only to keep order in the last resort.
Let us suppose a similar plan applied in Ireland.
There are four provinces there, forming four
natural wholes — or perhaps (if it should seem
expedient to put Munster and Connaught to-

gether) three. The Parliament of the empire
would still be in London, and Ireland would
send members to it. But at the same time each
Irish province would have its own legislature,
and the control of its own real affairs. The
British landlord would no longer determine the
dealings with land in an Irish province, nor the
British Protestant the dealings with church and
education. Apart from imperial concerns, or
from disorders such as to render military inter-
vention necessary, the government in London
would leave Ireland to manage itself. Lord
Spencer and Mr. Campbell Bannerman would
come back to England. Dublin Castle would
be the State House of Leinster. Land questions, game laws, police, church, education, would
be regulated by the people and legislature of
Leinster for Leinster, of Ulster for Ulster, of
Munster and Connaught for Munster and Connaught. The same with the like matters in
England and Scotland. The local legislatures
would regulate them.

But there is more. Everybody who watches
the working of our institutions perceives what
strain and friction is caused in it at present, by
our having a Second Chamber composed almost
entirely of great landowners, and representing
the feelings and interests of the class of land-

owners almost exclusively. No one, certainly, under the conditions of a modern age and our actual life, would ever think of devising such a Chamber. But we will allow ourselves to do more than merely state this truism, we will allow ourselves to ask what sort of Second Chamber, people who thought straight and saw clear would, under the conditions of a modern age and of our actual life, naturally make. And we find from the experience of the United States, that such provincial legislatures as we have just now seen to be the natural remedy for the confusion in the House of Commons, the natural remedy for the confusion in Ireland, have the further great merit, besides, of giving us the best basis possible for a modern Second Chamber. The United States Senate is per- haps, of all the institutions of that country, the most happily devised, the most successful in its working. The legislature of each State in the Union elects two senators to the Second Cham- ber of the national Congress at Washington. The senators are the Lords — if we like to keep, as it is surely best to keep, for designating the members of the Second Chamber, the title to which we have been for so many ages habitu- ated. Each of the provincial legislatures of Great Britain and Ireland would elect members

to the House of Lords. The colonial legislatures also would elect members to it ; and thus
we should be complying in the most simple and
yet the most signal way possible with the present desire of both this country and the colonies
for a closer union together, for some representation of the colonies in the Imperial Parliament. Probably, it would be found expedient
to transfer to the Second Chamber the representatives of the universities. But no scheme
for a Second Chamber will at the present day be
found solid unless it stands on a genuine basis
of election and representation. All schemes
for forming a Second Chamber through nomination, whether by the Crown or by any other
voice, of picked noblemen, great officials, leading merchants and bankers, eminent men of
letters and science, are fantastic. Probably,
they would not give us by any means a good
Second Chamber. But, certainly, they would
not satisfy the country or possess its confidence,
and therefore they would be found futile and
unworkable.

So we discover what would naturally appear
the desirable way out of some of our worst confusions, to anybody who saw clear and thought
straight. But there is little likelihood, probably,
of any such way being soon perceived and fol-

lowed by our community here. And why is this? Because, as a community, we have so little lucidity, we so little see clear and think straight. And why, again, is this? Because our community is so little homogeneous. The lower class has yet to show what it will do in politics. Rising politicians are already beginning to flatter it with servile assiduity, but their praise is as yet premature; the lower class is too little known. The upper class and the middle class we know. They have each their own supposed interests, and these are very different from the true interests of the community. Our very classes make us dim-seeing. In a modern time, we are living with a system of classes so intense, a society of such unnatural complication, that the whole action of our minds is hampered and falsened by it. I return to my old thesis: inequality is our bane. The great impediments in our way of progress are aristocracy and Protestant dissent. People think this is an epigram; alas, it is much rather a truism!

An aristocratical society like ours is often said to be the society from which artists and men of letters have most to gain. But an institution is to be judged, not by what one can oneself gain from it, but by the ideal which it sets up. An aristocracy — if I may once

more repeat words, which, however often re-
peated, have still a value, from their truth —
aristocracy now sets up in our country a false
ideal, which materializes our upper class, vul-
garizes our middle class, brutalizes our lower
class.   It misleads the young, makes the
worldly more worldly, the limited more limited,
the stationary more stationary.   Even to the
imaginative, whom Lord John Manners thinks
its sure friend, it is more a hindrance than a
help.   Johnson says well : " Whatever makes
the past, the distant, or the future, predominate
over the present, advances us in the dignity of
thinking beings."   But what is a Duke of Nor-
folk or an Earl of Warwick, dressed in broad-
cloth and tweed, and going about his business or
pleasure in hansom cabs and railway carriages,
like the rest of us ?   Imagination herself would
entreat him to take himself out of the way, and
to leave us to the Norfolks and Warwicks of
history.

I say this without a particle of hatred, and
with esteem, admiration, and affection for many
individuals in the aristocratical class.   But the
action of time and circumstance is fatal.   If
one asks oneself what is really to be desired,
what is expedient, one would go far beyond the
substitution of an elected Second Chamber for

the present House of Lords. All confiscation is to be reprobated, all deprivation (except in bad cases of abuse) of what is actually possessed. But one would wish, if one set about wishing, for the extinction of title, after the death of the holder, and for the dispersion of property by a stringent law of bequest. Our society should be homogeneous, and only in this way can it become so.

But aristocracy is in little danger. "I suppose, sir," a dissenting minister said to me, the other day, "you found, when you were in America, that they envied us there our great aristocracy." It was his sincere belief that they did, and such probably, is the sincere belief of our middle class in general ; or, at any rate, that if the Americans do not envy us this possession, they ought to. And my friend; one of the great Liberal party which has now, I suppose, pretty nearly run down its deceased wife's sister, poor thing, has his hand and heart full, so far as politics are concerned, of the question of church disestablishment. He is eager to set to work at a change which, even if it were desirable (and I think it is not), is yet off the line of those reforms which are really pressing.

Mr. Lyulph Stanley, Professor Stuart, and Lord Richard Grosvenor are waiting ready to

help him, and perhaps Mr. Chamberlain himself will lead the attack.   I admire Mr. Chamberlain as a politician, because he has the
courage — and it is a wise courage — to state
large the reforms we need, instead of mini-
mizing them.   But like Saul, before his con-
version, he breathes out threatenings and
slaughter against the Church, and is likely,
perhaps, to lead an assault upon her.   He is a
formidable assailant, yet I suspect he might
oreak his finger-nails on her walls.   If the
Church has the majority for her, she will of
course stand.   But in any case, this institution,
with all its faults, has that merit which makes
the great strength of institutions — it offers an
ideal which is noble and attaching.   Equality
is its profession, if not always its practice.   It
inspires wide and deep affection, and possesses,
therefore, immense strength.   Probably the
establishment will not stand in Wales probably
it will not stand in Scotland.   In Wales, it
ought not, I think, to stand.   In Scotland, I
should regret its fall : but Presbyterian churches
are born to separatism, as the sparks fly up-
wards.   At any rate, it is through the vote of
local legislatures that disestablishment is likely
to come, as a measure required in certain provinces, not as a general measure for the whole

country. In other words, the endeavor for disestablishment ought to be postponed to the
endeavor for far more important reforms, not
to precede it. Yet I doubt whether Mr.
Chamberlain and Mr. Lyulph Stanley will listen
to me when I plead thus with them; there is
so little lucidity in England, and they will say
I am priest-ridden.

One man there is, whom above all others I
would fain have seen in Parliament during the
last ten years, and beheld established in influence there at this juncture, — Mr. Goldwin
Smith. I do not say that he was not too em-
bittered against the Church; in my opinion he
was. But with singular lucidity and penetra-
tion he saw what great reforms were needed in
other directions, and the order of relative importance in which reforms stood. Such were
his character, style, and faculties, that alone perhaps among men of his insight he was capable
of getting his ideas weighed and entertained by
men in power; while amid all favor and under
all temptations he was certain to have still remained true to his insight, "unshaken, unse-
duced, unterrified." I think of him as a real
power for good in Parliament at this time, had
he by now become, as he might have become,
one of the leaders there. His absence from the

scene, his retirement in Canada, is a loss to his friends, but a still greater loss to his country.

Hardly inferior in influence to Parliament itself is journalism. I do not conceive of Mr. John Morley as made for filling that position in Parliament which Mr. Goldwin Smith would, I think, have filled. If he controls, as Protesilaos in the poem advises, hysterical passion (the besetting danger of men of letters on the platform and in Parliament) and remembers to approve "the depth and not the tumult of the soul," he will be powerful in Parliament; he will rise, he will come into office; but he will not do for us in Parliament, I think, what Mr. Goldwin Smith would have done. He is too much of a partisan. In journalism, on the other hand, he was as unique a figure as Mr. Goldwin Smith would, I imagine, have been in Parliament. As a journalist, Mr. John Morley showed a mind which seized and understood the signs of the times; he had all the ideas of a man of the best insight, and alone, perhaps, among men of his insight, he had the skill for making these ideas pass into journalism. But Mr. John Morley has now left journalism. There is plenty of talent in Parliament, plenty of talent in journalism, but no one in either to expound "the signs of this time" as these two men might have expounded them. The signs of the time, political and social, are left, I regret to say, to bring themselves as they best can to the notice of the public. Yet how ineffective an organ is literature for conveying them, compared with Parliament and journalism !

Conveyed somehow, however, they certainly should be, and in this disquisition I have tried to deal with them. But the political and social problem, as the thinkers call it, must not so occupy us as to make us forget the human problem. The problems are connected together, but they are not identical. Our political and social confusions I admit ; what Parliament is at this moment, I see and deplore. Yet nowhere but in England even now, not in France, not in Germany, not in America, could there be found public men of that quality — so capable of fair dealing, of trusting one another, keeping their word to one another — as to make possible such a settlement of the Franchise and Seats Bills as that which we have lately seen. Plato says with most profound truth : " The man who would think to good purpose must be able to take many things into his view together." How homogeneous American society is, I have done my best to declare ; how smoothly and naturally the institutions of the United States work, how

clearly, in some most important respects, the
Americans see, how straight they think.   Yet
. Sir Lepel Griffin says that there is no country
calling itself civilized where one would not
rather live than in America, except Russia.   In
politics I do not much trust Sir Lepel Griffin.
I hope that he administers in India some district where a profound insight into the being
and working of institutions is not requisite.
But, I suppose, of the tastes of himself and of
that large class of Englishmen whom Mr.
Charles Sumner has taught us to call the class
of gentlemen, he is no untrustworthy reporter.
And an Englishman of this class would rather
live in France, Spain, Holland, Belgium, Germany, Italy, Switzerland, than in the United
States, in spite of our community of race and
speech with them !   This means that, in the
opinion of men of that class, the human problem, at least, is not well solved in the United
States, whatever the political and social problem
may be.   And to the human problem in the
United States we ought certainly to turn our
attention, especially when we find taken such an
objection as this ; and some day, though not
now, we will do so, and try to see what the ob·
jection comes to.   I have given hostages to the
United States, I am bound to them by the

memory of great, untiring, and most attaching kindness. I should not like to have to own them to be of all countries calling themselves civilized, except Russia, the country where one would least like to live.

CIVILIZATION IN THE UNITED STATES.

IV.

CIVILIZATION IN THE UNITED STATES.

Two or three years ago I spoke in this Review * on the subject of America; and after considering the institutions and the social condition of the people of the United States, I said that what, in the jargon of the present day, is called "the political and social problem," does seem to be solved there with remarkable success. I pointed out the contrast which in this respect the United States offer to our own country, — a contrast, in several ways, much to their advantage. But I added that the solution of the political and social problem, as it is called, ought not so to absorb us as to make us forget the human problem; and that it remained to ask how the human problem is solved in the United States. It happened that Sir Lepel Griffin, a very acute and distinguished Indian official, had just then been travelling in the United States, and had published his opinion,

* *The Nineteenth Century*, London.

from what he saw of the life there, that there
is no country calling itself civilized where one
would not rather live than in America, except
Russia. Certainly then, I said, one cannot rest
satisfied, when one finds such a judgment passed
on the United States as this, with admiring
their institutions and their solid social condition,
their freedom and equality, their power, energy,
and wealth. One must, further, go on to exam-
ine what is done there towards solving the
human problem, and must see what Sir Lepel
Griffin's objection comes to.

And this examination I promised that I would
one day make. However, it is so delicate a
matter to discuss how a sensitive nation solves
the human problem, that I found myself inclined
to follow the example of the Greek moralist
Theophrastus, who waited, before composing
his famous *characters*, until he was ninety-nine
years old. I thought I had perhaps better wait
until I was about that age, before I discussed
the success of the Americans in solving the
human problem. But ninety-nine is a great
age ; it is probable that I may never reach it,
or even come near it. So I have determined,
finally, to face the question without any such
long delay, and thus I come to offer to the
readers of this Review the remarks following.

With the same frankness with which I discussed here the solution of the political and social problem by the people of the United States, I shall discuss their success in solving the human problem.

Perhaps it is not likely that any one will now remember what I said three years ago here about the success of the Americans in solving the political and social problem. I will sum it up in the briefest possible manner. I said that the United States had constituted themselves in a modern age; that their institutions complied well with the form and pressure of those circumstances and conditions which a modern age presents. Quite apart from all question how much of the merit for this may be due to the wisdom and virtue of the American people, and how much to their good fortune, it is undeniable that their institutions do work well and happily. The play of their institutions suggests, I said, the image of a man in a suit of clothes which fits him to perfection, leaving all his movements unimpeded and easy; a suit of clothes loose where it ought to be loose, and sitting close where its sitting close is an advantage; a suit of clothes able, moreover, to adapt itself naturally to the wearer's growth, and to admit of all enlargements as they successively arise.

So much as to the solution, by the United States, of the political problem. As to the social problem, I observed that the people of the United States were a community singularly free from the distinction of classes, singularly homogeneous ; that the division between rich and poor was consequently less profound there than in countries where the distinction of classes accentuates that division. I added that I believed there was exaggeration in the reports of their administrative and judicial corruption ; and altogether, I concluded, the United States, politically and socially, are a country living prosperously in a natural modern condition, and conscious of living prosperously in such a condition. And being in this healthy case, and having this healthy consciousness, the community there uses its understanding with the soundness of health ; it in general, as to its own political and social concerns, sees clear and thinks straight. Comparing the United States with ourselves, I said that while they are in this natural and healthy condition, we, on the contrary, are so little homogeneous, we are living with a system of classes so intense, with institutions and a society so little modern, so unnaturally complicated, that the whole action of our minds is hampered and falsened by it ; we are in consequence wanting in lucidity, we do not see clear or think straight, and the Americans have here much the advantage of us.

Yet we find an acute and experienced Englishman saying that there is no country, calling itself civilized, where one would not rather live than in the United States, except Russia! The civilization of the United States must somehow, if an able man can think thus, have shortcomings, in spite of the country's success and prosperity. What is civilization? It is the humanization of man in society, the satisfaction for him, in society, of the true law of human nature. Man's study, says Plato, is to discover the right answer to the question *how to live?* our aim, he says, is very and true life. We are more or less civilized as we come more or less near to this aim, in that social state which the pursuit of our aim essentially demands. But several elements or powers, as I have often insisted, go to build up a complete human life. There is the power of conduct, the power of intellect and knowledge, the power of beauty, the power of social life and manners; we have instincts responding to them all, requiring them all. And we are perfectly civilized only when all these instincts in our nature, all these elements in our civilization, have been adequately recognized and satisfied. But of course this adequate recognition and satisfaction of all the elements in question is impossible ; some of them are recognized more than others, some of them more in one community, some in another ; and the satisfactions found are more or less worthy.

And, meanwhile, people use the term *civiliza-tion* in the loosest possible way, for the most part attaching to it, however, in their own mind some meaning connected with their own preferences and experiences. The most common meaning thus attached to it is perhaps that of a satisfaction, not of all the main demands of human nature, but of the demand for the comforts and conveniences of life, and of this demand as made by the sort of person who uses the term.

Now we should always attend to the common and prevalent use of an important term. Probably Sir Lepel Griffin had this notion of the comforts and conveniences of life much in his thoughts when he reproached American civili-zation with its shortcomings. For men of his kind, and for all that large number of men, so prominent in this country and who make their voice so much heard, men who have been at the public schools and universities, men of the

professional and official class, men who do the
most part of our literature and our journalism,
America is not a comfortable place of abode.
A man of this sort has in England everything
in his favor; society appears organized expressly for his advantage. A Rothschild or a
Vanderbilt can buy his way anywhere, and can
have what comforts and luxuries he likes,
whether in America or in England. But it is
in England that an income of from three or
four to fourteen or fifteen hundred a year does
so much for its possessor, enables him to live
with so many of the conveniences of far richer
people. For his benefit, his benefit above all,
clubs are organized and hansom cabs ply;
service is abundant, porters stand waiting at
the railway stations. In America all luxuries
are dear except oysters and ice; service is in
general scarce and bad; a club is a most expensive luxury: the cab-rates are prohibitive —
more than half of the people who in England
would use cabs must in America use the horse-
cars, the tram. The charges of tailors and
mercers are about a third higher than they are
with us. I mention only a few striking points
as to which there can be no dispute, and in
which a man of Sir Lepel Griffin's class would
feel the great difference between America and

England in the conveniences at his command.
There are a hundred other points one might
mention, where he would feel the same thing.
When a man is passing judgment on a country's civilization, points of this kind crowd to
his memory, and determine his sentence.

On the other hand, for that immense class of
people, the great bulk of the community, the
class of people whose income is less than three
or four hundred a year, things in America are
favorable. It is easier for them there than in
the Old World to rise and to make their fortune;
but I am not now speaking of that. Even without making their fortune, even with their
income below three or four hundred a year,
things are favorable to them in America, society
seems organized there for their benefit. To
begin with, the humbler kind of work is better
paid in America than with us; the higher kind,
worse. The official, for instance, gets less, his
office-keeper gets more. The public ways are
abominably cut up by rails and blocked with
horse-cars; but the inconvenience is for those
who use private carriages and cabs, the convenience is for the bulk of the community who
but for the horse-cars would have to walk.
The ordinary railway cars are not delightful,
but they are cheap, and they are better fur-

nished and in winter are warmer than third-class carriages in England. Luxuries are, as I have said, very dear — above all, European luxuries; but a working-man's clothing is nearly as cheap as in England, and plain food is on the whole cheaper. Even luxuries of a certain kind are within a laboring man's easy reach. I have mentioned ice; I will mention fruit also. The abundance and cheapness of fruit is a great boon to people of small incomes in America. Do not believe the Americans when they extol their peaches as equal to any in the world, or better than any in the world; they are not to be compared to peaches grown under glass. Do not believe that the American Newtown pippins appear in the New York and Boston fruit-shops as they appear in those of London and Liverpool ; or that the Americans have any pear to give you like the Marie Louise. But what laborer, or artisan, or small clerk, ever gets hot-house peaches, or Newtown pippins, or Marie Louise pears? Not such good pears, apples, and peaches as those, but pears, apples, and peaches by no means to be despised, such people and their families do in America get in plenty.

Well, now, what would a philosopher or a philanthropist say in this case? which would he say was the more civilized condition — that of the country where the balance of advantage, as to the comforts and conveniences of life, is greatly in favor of the people with incomes below three hundred a year, or that of the country where it is greatly in favor of those with incomes above that sum?

Many people will be ready to give an answer to that question without the smallest hesitation. They will say that they are, and that all of us ought to be, for the greatest happiness of the greatest number.   However, the question is not one which I feel bound now to discuss and answer.   Of course, if happiness and civilization consists in being plentifully supplied with the comforts and conveniences of life, the question presents little difficulty.   But I believe neither that happiness consists, merely or mainly, in being plentifully supplied with the comforts and conveniences of life, nor that civilization consists in being so supplied; therefore, I leave the question unanswered.

I prefer to seek for some other and better tests by which to try the civilization of the United States.   I have often insisted on the need of more equality in our own country, and on the mischiefs caused by inequality over here. In the United States there is not our intense

division of classes, our inequality ; there is great
equality. Let me mention two points in the
system of social life and manners over there in
which this equality seems to me to have done
good. The first is a mere point of form, but it
has its significance. Every one knows it is the
established habit with us in England, if we write
to people supposed to belong to the class of
gentlemen, of addressing them by the title of
Esquire, while we keep *Mr.* for people not supposed to belong to that clsss. If we think of it,
could one easily find a habit more ridiculous,
more offensive ? The title of *Esquire,* like most
of our titles, comes out of the great frippery
shop of the Middle Age ; it is alien to the sound
taste and manner of antiquity, when men said
Pericles and *Camillus.* But unlike other titles,
it is applied or withheld quite arbitrarily.
Surely, where a man has no specific title proper
to him, the one plain title of *Master* or *Mr.* is
enough, and we need not be encumbered with a
second title of *Esquire,* now quite unmeaning,
to draw an invidious and impossible line of distinction between those who are gentlemen and
those who are not ; as if we actually wished to
provide a source of embarrassment for the
sender of a letter, and of mortification for the
receiver of it.

The French, those great authorities in social life and manners, find *Mr.* enough, and the Americans are more and more, I am glad to say, following the French example. I only hope they will persevere, and not be seduced by *Esquire* being "so English, you know." And I do hope, moreover, that we shall one day take the same course and drop our absurd *Esquire*.

The other point goes deeper. Much may be said against the voices and intonation of American women. But almost every one acknowledges that there is a charm in American women — a charm which you find in almost all of them, wherever you go. It is the charm of a natural manner, a manner not self-conscious, artificial, and constrained. It may not be a beautiful manner always, but it is almost always a natural manner, a free and happy manner; and this gives pleasure. Here we have, undoubtedly, a note of civilization, and an evidence, at the same time, of the good effect of equality upon social life and manners. I have often heard it observed that a perfectly natural manner is as rare among Englishwomen of the middle classes as it is general among American women of like condition with them. And so far as the observation is true, the reason of its truth no doubt is, that the Englishwoman is living in presence of

an upper class, as it is called — in presence,
that is, of a class of women recognized as being
the right thing in style and manner, and whom
she imagines criticising *her* style and manner,
finding this or that to be amiss with it, this or
that to be vulgar. Hence, self-consciousness and
constraint in her. The American woman lives
in presence of no such class ; there may be circles trying to pass themselves off as such a class,
giving themselves airs as such, but they command no recognition, no authority. The American woman in general is perfectly unconcerned
about their opinion, is herself, enjoys her existence, and has, consequently, a manner happy and
natural. It is her great charm ; and it is moreover, as I have said, a real note of civilization,
and one which has to be reckoned to the credit
of American life, and of its equality.

But we must get nearer still to the heart of
the question raised as to the character and worth
of American civilization. I have said how much
the word civilization really means — the humanization of man in society ; his making progress
there towards his true and full humanity. Partial and material achievement is always being
put forward as civilization. We hear a nation
called highly civilized by reason of its industry,
commerce, and wealth, or by reason of its liberty

or equality, or by reason of its numerous
churches, schools, libraries, and newspapers.
But there is something in human nature, some
instinct of growth, some law of perfection,
which rebels against this narrow account of the
matter. And perhaps what human nature
demands in civilization, over and above all those
obvious things which first occur to our thoughts,
— what human nature, I say, demands in civilization, if it is to stand as a high and satisfying
civilization, is best described by the word *interesting.* Here is the extraordinary charm of the
old Greek civilization : that it is so *interesting.*
Do not tell me only, says human nature, of the
magnitude of your industry and commerce ; of
the beneficence of your institutions, your freedom, your equality ; of the great and growing
number of your churches and schools, libraries
and newpapers ; tell me also if your civilization
— which is the grand name you give to all this
development — tell me if your civilization is
interesting.

An American friend of mine, Professor Nor-
ton, has lately published the early letters of
Carlyle. If any one wants a good antidote to
the unpleasant effect left by Mr. Froude's " Life
of Carlyle," let him read those letters. Not
only of Carlyle will those letters make him

think kindly, but they will also fill him with admiring esteem for the qualities, character, and family life, as there delineated, of the Scottish peasant. Well, the Carlyle family were numerous, poor, and struggling. Thomas Carlyle, the eldest son, a young man in wretched health and worse spirits, was fighting his way in Edinburgh. One of his younger brothers talked of emigrating. "The very best thing he could do!" we should all say. Carlyle dissuades him. "You shall never," he writes, "you shall never seriously meditate crossing the great Salt Pool to plant yourself in the Yankee-land. That is a miserable fate for any one, at best ; never dream of it. Could you banish yourself from all that is interesting to your mind, forget the history, the glorious institutions, the noble principles of old Scotland — that you might eat a better dinner, perhaps ?"

There is our word launched — the word *interesting*. I am not saying that Carlyle's advice was good, or that young men should not emigrate. I do but take note, in the word *interesting*, of a requirement, a cry of aspiration, a cry not sounding in the imaginative Carlyle's own breast only, but sure of a response in his brother's breast also, and in human nature.

Amiel, that contemplative Swiss whose jour-

nals the world has been reading lately, tells us
that "the human heart is, as it were, haunted
by confused reminiscences of an age of gold ;
or, rather, by aspirations towards a harmony of
things which every day reality denies to us."
He says that the splendor and refinement of
high life is an attempt by the rich and cultivated classes to realize this ideal, and is "a
form of poetry." And the interest which this
attempt awakens in the classes which are not
rich or cultivated, their indestructible interest
in the pageant and fairy tale, as to them it
appears, of the life in castles and palaces, the
life of the great, bears witness to a like imaginative strain in them also, a strain tending after
the elevated and the beautiful. In short, what
Goethe describes as "was uns alle bändigt, *das
Gemeine*—that which holds us all in bondage,
the common and ignoble," is, notwithstanding
its admitted prevalence, contrary to a deep-
seated instinct of human nature, and repelled
by it. Of civilization, which is to humanize us
in society, we demand, before we will consent
to be satisfied with it — we demand, however
much else it may give us, that it shall give us,
too, the *interesting*.

Now, the great sources of the *interesting* are
distinction and beauty: that which is elevated,

and that which is beautiful. Let us take the
beautiful first, and consider how far it is present
in American civilization. Evidently, this is that
civilization's weak side. There is little to nour-
ish and delight the sense of beauty there. In
the long-settled states east of the Alleghanies
the landscape in general is not interesting, the
climate harsh and in extremes. The Americans
are restless, eager to better themselves and to
make fortunes; the inhabitant does not strike
his roots lovingly down into the soil, as in rural
England. In the valley of the Connecticut you
will find farm after farm which the Yankee set-
tler has abandoned in order to go West, leaving
the farm to some new Irish immigrant. The
charm of beauty which comes from ancientness
and permanence of rural life the country could
not yet have in a high degree, but it has it in
an even less degree than might be expected.
Then the Americans come originally, for the
most part, from that great class in English
society amongst whom the sense for conduct
and business is much more strongly developed
than the sense for beauty. If we in England
were without the cathedrals, parish churches,
and castles of the catholic and feudal age, and
without the houses of the Elizabethan age, but
had only the towns and buildings which the rise

of our middle class has created in the modern age, we should be in much the same case as the Americans. We should be living with much the same absence of training for the sense of beauty through the eye, from the aspect of outward things. The American cities have hardly anything to please a trained or a natural sense for beauty. They have buildings which cost a great deal of money and produce a certain effect — buildings, shall I say, such as our Midland Station at St. Pancras; but nothing such as Somerset House or Whitehall. One architect of genius they had — Richardson. I had the pleasure to know him : he is dead, alas! Much of his work was injured by the conditions under which he was obliged to execute it ; I can recall but one building, and that of no great importance, where he seems to have had his own way, to be fully himself ; but that is indeed excellent. In general, where the Americans succeed best in their architecture — in that art so indicative and educative of a people's sense for beauty — is in the fashion of their villa-cottages in wood. These are often original and at the same time very pleasing, but they are pretty and coquettish, not beautiful. Of the really beautiful in the other arts, and in literature, very little has been produced there as yet. I asked a German portrait-painter, whom I found painting and prospering in America, how he liked the country. "How *can* an artist like it?" was his answer. The American artists live chiefly in Europe; all Americans of cultivation and wealth visit Europe more and more constantly. The mere nomenclature of the country acts upon a cultivated person like the incessant pricking of pins. What people in whom the sense for beauty and fitness was quick could have invented, or could tolerate, the hideous names ending in *ville*, the Briggsvilles, Higginsvilles, Jacksonvilles, rife from Maine to Florida; the jumble of unnatural and inappropriate names everywhere? On the line from Albany to Buffalo you have, in one part, half the names in the classical dictionary to designate the stations; it is said that the folly is due to a surveyor who, when the country was laid out, happened to possess a classical dictionary; but a people with any artist-sense would have put down that surveyor. The Americans meekly retain his names; and, indeed, his strange Marcellus or Syracuse is perhaps not much worse than their congenital Briggsville.

So much as to beauty, and as to the provision, in the United States, for the sense of beauty. As to distinction, and the interest which human

nature seeks from enjoying the effect made upon it by what is elevated, the case is much the
same.   There is very little to create such an
effect, very much to thwart it.   Goethe says
somewhere that " the thrill of awe is the best
thing humanity has " : —

Das Schaudern ist der Menschheit bestes Theil.

But, if there be a discipline in which the Americans are wanting, it is the discipline of awe and
respect.   An austere and intense religion im-
posed on their Puritan founders the discipline of
respect, and so provided for them the thrill of
awe ; but this religion is dying out.   The
Americans have produced plenty of men strong,
shrewd, upright, able, effective ; very few who
are highly distinguished.   Alexander Hamilton
is indeed a man of rare distinction ; Washington, though he has not the high mental distinction of Pericles or Cæsar, has true distinction
of style and character.   But these men belong
to the pre-American age.   Lincoln's recent
American biographers declare that Washington
is but an Englishman, an English officer ; the
typical American, they say, is Abraham Lincoln.   Now Lincoln is shrewd, sagacious, hu-
morous, honest, courageous, firm ; he is a man

with qualities deserving the most sincere esteem and praise, but he has not distinction.

In truth, everything is against distinction in
America, and against the sense of elevation to
be gained through admiring and respecting it.
The glorification of "the average man," who is
quite a religion with statesmen and publicists
there, is against it. The addiction to "the
funny man," who is a national misfortune there,
is against it. Above all, the newspapers are
against it.

It is often said that every nation has the government it deserves. What is much more certain is that every nation has the newspapers it
deserves. The newspaper is the direct product
of the want felt ; the supply answers closely and
inevitably to the demand. I suppose no one
knows what the American newspapers are, who
has not been obliged, for some length of time,
to read either those newspapers or none at all.
Powerful and valuable contributions occur scattered about in them. But on the whole, and
taking the total impression and effect made by
them, I should say that if one were searching
for the best means to efface and kill in a whole
nation the discipline of respect, the feeling for
what is elevated, one could not do better than
take the American newspapers. The absence

of truth and soberness in them, the poverty in
serious interest, the personality and sensation-
mongering, are beyond belief.   There are a
few newspapers which are in whole, or in part,
exceptions.   The *New York Nation*, a weekly
paper, may be paralleled with the *Saturday
Review* as it was in its old and good days ; but
the *New York Nation* is conducted by a for-
eigner, and has an extremely small sale.   In
general, the daily papers are such that when one
returns home one is moved to admiration and
thankfulness not only at the great London papers, like the *Times* or the *Standard*, but quite
as much at the great provincial newspapers, too,
— papers like the *Leeds Mercury* and the *York-
shire Post* in the north of England, like the
Scotsman and the *Glasgow Herald* in Scotland.

The Americans used to say to me that what
they valued was news, and that this their newspapers gave them.   I at last made the reply: " Yes,
news for the servants' hall ! "   I remember that
a New York newspaper, one of the first I saw
after landing in the country, had a long account,
with the prominence we should give to the illness of the German Emperor or the arrest of
the Lord Mayor of Dublin, of a young woman
who had married a man who was a bag of bones,
as we say, and who used to exhibit himself as a

skeleton ; of her growing horror in living with this man, and finally of her death. All this in the most minute detail, and described with all the writer's powers of rhetoric. This has always remained by me as a specimen of what the Americans call news.

You must have lived amongst their newspapers to know what they are. If I relate some of my own experiences, it is because these will give a clear enough notion of what the newspapers over there are, and one remembers more definitely what has happened to oneself. Soon after arriving in Boston, I opened a Boston newspaper and came upon a column headed: "Tickings." By *tickings* we are to understand news conveyed through the tickings of the telegraph. The first "ticking" was : "Matthew Arnold is sixty-two years old" — an age, I must just say in passing, which I had not then reached. The second "ticking" was : "Wales says, Mary is a darling"; the meaning being that the Prince of Wales expressed great admiration for Miss Mary Anderson. This was at Boston, the American Athens. I proceeded to Chicago. An evening paper was given me soon after I arrived ; I opened it, and found under a large-type heading, " *We have seen him arrive*," the following picture of myself : " He

has harsh features, supercilious manners, parts
his hair down the middle, wears a single eye-
glass and ill-fitting clothes." Notwithstanding
this rather unfavorable introduction, I was most
kindly and hospitably received at Chicago. It
happened that I had a letter for Mr. Medill, an
elderly gentleman of Scotch descent, the editor
of the chief newspaper in those parts, the *Chicago Tribune.* I called on him, and we con-
versed amicably together. Some time afterwards, when I had gone back to England, a
New York paper published a criticism of Chicago and its people, purporting to have been
contributed by me to the *Pall Mall Gazette*
over here. It was a poor hoax, but many people were taken in and were excusably angry.
Mr. Medill of the *Chicago Tribune* amongst the
number. A friend telegraphed to me to know
if I had written the criticism. I, of course, instantly telegraphed back that I had not written
a syllable of it. Then a Chicago paper is sent
to me ; and what I have the pleasure of reading,
as the result of my contradiction, is this : "Arnold denies ; Mr. Medill [my old friend] refuses
to accept Arnold's disclaimer ; says Arnold is a
cur."

I once declared that in England the born
lover of ideas and of light could not but feel

that the sky over his head is of brass and iron.
And so I say that, in America, he who craves
for the *interesting* in civilization, he who requires from what surrounds him satisfaction for
his sense of beauty, his sense for elevation, will
feel the sky over his head to be of brass and
iron.   The human problem, then, is as yet
solved in the United States most imperfectly;
a great void exists in the civilization over there;
a want of what is elevated and beautiful, of
what is interesting.

The want is grave; it was probably, though
he does not exactly bring it out, influencing Sir
Lepel Griffin's feelings when he said that America is one of the last countries in which one
would like to live.   The want is such as to
make any educated man feel that many countries, much less free and prosperous than the
United States, are yet more truly civilized;
have more which is interesting, have more to
say to the soul; are countries, therefore, in
which one would rather live.

The want is graver because it is so little recognized by the mass of Americans; nay, so
loudly denied by them.   If the community over
there perceived the want and regretted it, sought
for the right ways of remedying it, and resolved
that remedied it should be; if they said, or

even if a number of leading spirits amongst
them said : " Yes, we see what is wanting to
our civilization, we see that the average man is
a danger, we see that our newspapers are a
scandal, that bondage to the common and ignoble is our snare ; but under the circumstances
our civilization could not well have been expected to begin differently.   What you see are
beginnings, they are crude, they are too pre-
dominantly material, they omit much, leave
much to be desired — but they could not have
been otherwise, they have been inevitable, and
we will rise above them "; if the Americans
frankly said this, one would have not a word to
bring against it.   One would *then* insist on no
shortcoming, one would accept their admission
that the human problem is at present quite in-
sufficiently solved by them, and would press the
matter no further.   One would congratulate
them on having solved the political problem
and the social problem so successfully, and only
remark, as I have said already, that in seeing
clear and thinking straight on *our* political and
social questions, we have great need to follow
the example they set us on theirs.

But now the Americans seem, in certain matters, to have agreed, as a people, to deceive
themselves, to persuade themselves that they

have what they have not, to cover the defects
in their civilization by boasting, to fancy that
they well and truly solve, not only the political
and social problem, but the human problem too.
One would say that they do really hope to find
in tall talk and inflated sentiment a substitute
for that real sense of elevation which human
nature, as I have said, instinctively craves —
and a substitute which may do as well as the
genuine article. The thrill of awe, which Goethe
pronounces to be the best thing humanity has,
they would fain create by proclaiming themselves at the top of their voices to be "the
greatest nation upon earth," by assuring one
another, in the language of their national his-
torian, that "American democracy proceeds in
its ascent as uniformly and majestically as the
laws of being, and is as certain as the decrees
of eternity."

Or, again, far from admitting that their newspapers are a scandal, they assure one another
that their newspaper press is one of their most
signal distinctions. Far from admitting that in
literature they have as yet produced little that
is important, they play at treating American
literature as if it were a great independent
power; they reform the spelling of the English
language by the insight of their average man.

For every English writer they have an American
writer to match ; and him good Americans read.
The Western States are at this moment being
nourished and formed, we hear, on the novels
of a native author called Roe, instead of those
of Scott and Dickens.   Far from admitting that
their average man is a danger, and that his predominance has brought about a plentiful lack of
refinement, distinction, and beauty, they declare
in the words of my friend Colonel Higginson, a
prominent critic at Boston, that "Nature said,
some years since: 'Thus far the English is my
best race, but we have had Englishmen enough ;
put in one drop more of nervous fluid and make
the American.'"   And with that drop a new
range of promise opened on the human race,
and a lighter, finer, more highly organized type
of mankind was born.   Far from admitting that
the American accent, as the pressure of their
climate and of their average man has made it,
is a thing to be striven against, they assure one
another that it is the right accent, the standard
English speech of the future.   It reminds me
of a thing in Smollet's dinner-party of authors.
Seated by "the philosopher who is writing a
most orthodox refutation of Bolingbroke, but in
the meantime has just been presented to the
Grand Jury as a public nuisance for having

blasphemed in an alehouse on the Lord's day "
— seated by this philosopher is "the Scotchman who is giving lectures on the pronunciation
of the English language."

The worst of it is, that all this tall talk and
self-glorification meets with hardly any rebuke
from sane criticism over there. I will mention,
in regard to this, a thing which struck me a
good deal. A Scotchman who has made a
great fortune at Pittsburg, a kind friend of
mine, one of the most hospitable and generous of men, Mr. Andrew Carnegie, published
a year or two ago a book called " Triumphant
Democracy," a most splendid picture of American progress. The book is full of valuable
information, but religious people thought that
it insisted too much on mere material progress,
and did not enough set forth America's deficiencies and dangers. And a friendly clergy-
man in Massachusetts, telling me how he regretted this, and how apt the Americans are
to shut their eyes to their own dangers, put
into my hands a volume written by a leading
minister among the Congregationalists, a very
prominent man, which he said supplied a good
antidote to my friend Mr. Carnegie's book.
The volume is entitled " Our Country." I read
it through. The author finds in evangelical

Protestanism, as the orthodox Protestant sects present it, the grand remedy for the deficiencies and dangers of America. On this I offer no criticism ; what struck me, and that on which I wish to lay stress, is, the writer's entire failure to perceive that such self-glorification and self-deception as I have been mentioning is one of America's dangers, or even that it *is* self-deception at all. He himself shares in all the self-deception of the average man among his countrymen ; he flatters it. In the very points where a serious critic would find the Americans most wanting he finds them superior ; only they require to have a good dose of evangelical Protestantism still added. " Ours is the elect nation," preaches this reformer of American faults — " ours is the elect nation for the age to come. We are the chosen people." Already, says he, we are taller and heavier than other men, longer lived than other men, richer and more energetic than other men, above all, "of finer nervous organization " than other men. Yes, this people, who endure to have the American newspaper for their daily reading, and to have their habitation in Briggsville, Jacksonville, and Marcellus — this people is of finer, more delicate nervous organization than other nations ! It is Colonel Higginson's " drop more of nervous

fluid," over again. This "drop" plays a stupen-
dous part in the American rhapsody of self-praise.
Undoubtedly the Americans are highly nervous, /
both the men and the women. A great Paris
physician says that he notes a distinct new
form of nervous disease, produced in American
women by worry about servants. But this nervousness, developed in the race out there by
worry, overwork, want of exercise, injudicious
diet, and a most trying climate — this morbid
nervousness, our friends ticket as the fine sus-
ceptibility of genius, and cite it as a proof of
their distinction, of their superior capacity for
civilization ! " The roots of civilization are the
nerves," says our Congregationalist instructor,
again ; "and, other things being equal, the
finest nervous organization will produce the
highest civilization. Now, the finest nervous
organization is ours."

The new West promises to beat in the game
of brag even the stout champions I have been
quoting. Those belong to the old Eastern
States ; and the other day there was sent to
me a Californian newspaper which calls all the
Easterners "the unhappy denizens of a forbid-
ding clime," and adds : " The time will surely
come when all roads will lead to California.
Here will be the home of art, science, literature, and profound knowledge."

Common-sense criticism, I repeat, of all this
hollow stuff there is in America next to none.
There are plenty of cultivated, judicious, delightful individuals there. They are our hope
and America's hope ; it is through their means
that improvement must come. They know perfectly well how false and hollow the boastful
stuff talked is ; but they let the storm of self-
laudation rage, and say nothing. For political
opponents and their doings there are in America
hard words to be heard in abundance ; for the
real faults in American civilization, and for the
foolish boasting which prolongs them, there is
hardly a word of regret or blame, at least in
public. Even in private, many of the most cultivated Americans shrink from the subject, are
irritable and thin-skinned when it is canvassed.
Public treatment of it, in a cool and sane spirit
of criticism, there is none. In vain I might
plead that I had set a good example of frankness, in confessing over here, that, so far from
solving our problems successfully, we in England find ourselves with an upper class materialized, a middle class vulgarized, and a lower
class brutalized. But it seems that nothing
will embolden an American critic to say firmly
and aloud to his countrymen and to his newspapers, that in America they do not solve the

human problem successfully, and that with their present methods they never can. Consequently, the masses of the American people do really come to believe all they hear about their finer nervous organization, and the rightness of the American accent, and the importance of American literature; that is to say, they see things not as they are, but as they would like them to be; they deceive themselves totally. And by such self-deception they shut against themselves the door to improvement, and do their best to make the reign of *das Gemeine* eternal. In what concerns the solving of the political and social problem they see clear and think straight; in what concerns the higher civilization they live in a fools' paradise. This it is which makes a famous French critic speak of "the hard unintelligence of the people of the United States" — *la dure inintelligence des Américains du Nord* — of the very people who in general pass for being specially intelligent; and so, within certain limits, they are. But they have been so plied with nonsense and boasting that outside those limits, and where it is a question of things in which their civilization is weak, they seem, very many of them, as if in such things they had no power of perception whatever, no idea of a proper scale, no sense of the difference between good and bad. And at this rate they can never, after solving the political and social problem with success, go on to solve happily the human problem too, and thus at last to make their civilization full and interesting.

To sum up, then.   What really dissatisfies in American civilization is the want of the *interesting*, a want due chiefly to the want of those two great elements of the interesting, which are elevation and beauty.   And the want of these elements is increased and prolonged by the Americans being assured that they have them when they have them not.   And it seems to me that what the Americans now most urgently require, is not so much a vast additional development of orthodox Protestantism, but rather a steady exhibition of cool and sane criticism by their men of light and leading over there.   And perhaps the very first step of such men should be to insist on having for America, and to create if need be, better newspapers.

To us, too, the future of the United States is of incalculable importance. Already we feel their influence much, and we shall feel it more. We have a good deal to learn from them ; we shall find in them, also, many things to beware of, many points in which it is to be hoped our democracy may not be like theirs. As our country becomes more democratic, the malady here may no longer be that we have an upper class materialized, a middle class vulgarized, and a lower class brutalized. But the predominance of the common and ignoble, born of the predominance of the average man, is a malady too. That the common and ignoble is human nature's enemy, that, of true human nature, distinction and beauty are needs, that a civilization is insufficient where these needs are not satisfied, faulty where they are thwarted, is an instruction of which we, as well as the Americans, may greatly require to take fast hold, and not to let go. We may greatly require to keep, as if it were our life, the doctrine that we are failures after all, if we cannot eschew vain boasting and vain imaginations, — eschew what flatters in us the common and ignoble, and approve things that are truly excellent.

I have mentioned evangelical Protestantism. There is a text which evangelical Protestantism — and, for that matter, Catholicism too — translates wrong and takes in a sense too narrow. The text is that well-known one, " except a man be born again, he cannot see the kingdom of God." Instead of *again*, we ought to translate *from above;* and instead of taking the kingdom of God in the sense of a life in Heaven above, we ought to take it, as its speaker meant it, in the sense of the reign of saints, a renovated and perfected human society on earth, — the ideal society of the future.   In the life of such a society, in the life *from above*, the life born of inspiration or *the spirit* — in that life elevation and beauty are not everything; but they are much, and they are indispensable. Humanity cannot reach its ideal while it lacks them, "Except a man be born *from above*, he cannot have part in the society of the future."

Important New Books.

STRAY LEAVES FROM NEWPORT. By Mrs. Wm. Lamont

WHEELER. *Exquisitely printed and most beautifully bound in tapestry, white and gold.* Gilt top. Uncut edges. 12mo. $1.50.

Two editions of these charming prose idyls were exhausted within two weeks of publication. Third edition now preparing.

The author is familiar with every detail of the social life of Newport, in which she has long been a prominent figure, and the types of character she presents will be readily recognized as direct copies from nature. She is intimately acquainted with the scenes she describes, and the literary quality of her book is of a character that will recommend it to readers of cultivated tastes. — Gazette.

IONA : A Lay of Ancient Greece. By Payne Erskine. Cr. 8vo. Cloth.

Gilt top. $1.75.

Musical, and full of classic beauty, recalling in many passages the delicate and subtle charm of Keats.

WHAT SHALL MAKE US WHOLE? or, Thoughts in the Direc-

tion of Man's Spiritual and Physical Integrity. By Helen Bigelow
MERRIMAN. *Third Edition.* 16mo, *unique boards.* 75 cents.

An endeavor to present in a popular way the philosophy and practice of mental healing.

The author does not claim for her essay either completeness or permanent value, but hopes "to fix a few points and establish a few relative values, in anticipation of the time when human research and experience shall complete the pictures."

She holds that the human mind can achieve nothing that is so good except when it becomes the channel of the infinite spirit of God, and that so-called mind cures are not brought about wholly by the power of the mind over the body, or by the influence of one mind over another.

Religious enthusiasm and scientific medicine abound in cases of extraordinary cures of diseases effected by what, for the sake of convenience, is generally called "faith."

It will not do, says the *British Medical Journal,* for pathologists and psychologists to treat these "modern miracles" so cavalierly.

In them are exhibited, in a more or less legitimate manner, the results of the action of the mind upon the bodily functions and particles.

Hysteria is curable by these phenomena, since hysteria, after all, is only an unhealthy mastery of the body over the mind, and is cured by this or any other stimulus to the imagination. "Therefore," says the editor of the above journal, "there is no reason to doubt that faith-healing, so called, may have more positive results than we have been accustomed to allow."

TYPICAL NEW ENGLAND ELMS AND OTHER TREES.

Reproduced by Photogravure from photographs by Henry Brooks, with an Introduction, and with Notes by L. L. Dame. 4to. [*In press.*]

Cupples and Hurd,   *Publishers,*
Booksellers,   BOSTON.
Library Agents,

THE FOUR GOSPELS. Translated into Modern English from the Authorized and Revised Versions. By ERNEST BILTON. Cloth. $1.00.

A cheap edition of a new translation of the Gospels, having a great run of popularity in the religious circles of Great Britain.

The author has taken the authorised version as it stands, availing himself of many corrections suggested by the revised version, and has given the apparent meaning of the text in the *plainest possible* language, the whole object being the simplification of the narratives of the Evangelists. It is not expected that this rendering will supersede the accepted version. The author *evidently feels* that he is not without hope that it may lead to the serious consideration, in proper quarters, of the advisability of providing the people with an authorised translation of the Scriptures into the "vulgar tongue," not of the *sixteenth* but of the *nineteenth* century.

THE SKETCHES OF THE CLANS OF SCOTLAND, with twenty-two full-page colored plates of Tartans. By CLANSMEN J. M. P. - F. W. S. Large 8vo. Cloth, $2.00.

The object of this treatise is to give a concise account of the origin, seat, and characteristics of the Scottish clans, together with a representation of the distinguishing tartan worn by each. *The illustrations are fine specimens of color work, all executed in Scotland.*

THE GREEN HAND; or, the Adventures of a Naval Lieutenant. A Sea Story. By GEORGE CUPPLES. With Portrait of the Author and other Illustrations. 1 vol. 12mo. Cloth. $2.00.

A new library edition of this fascinating sea classic. *[In press.*

ALL MATTER TENDS TO ROTATION, OR THE ORIGIN OF ENERGY. A New Hypothesis which throws Light upon all the Phenomena of Nature. Electricity, Magnetism, Gravitation, Light, Heat, and Chemical Action explained upon Mechanical Principles and traced to a Single Source. By LEONIDAS LE CENCI HAMILTON, M. A. Vol. 1. Origin of Energy: Electrostatics and Magnetism. Containing 100 Illustrations, including Fine Steel Portraits of Faraday and Maxwell. Handsomely bound in cloth. 8vo, 340 pp. Price, $3.00. *Net.*

In this volume the author has utilized the modern conception of lines of force originated by Faraday, and afterwards developed mathematically by Prof. J. Clerk Maxwell, and he has reached an explanation of electrical and magnetic phenomena which has been expected by physicists on both continents. It may have a greater influence upon the scientific world than either Newton's "Principia" or Darwin's "Origin of Species," because it places natural science upon its only true basis — Pure Mechanics.

Cupples and Hurd,   *Publishers,*
                        Booksellers,   *BOSTON.*
                        Library Agents,

Important New Books.

HOW TO WRITE THE HISTORY OF A FAMILY. By W. P.
W. PHILLIMORE, M. A., B. C. L.   1 vol.   Cr. 8vo.   *Tastefully printed in antique style, handsomely bound.* $2.00.

Unassuming, practical, essentially useful, Mr. Phillimore's book should be in the hands of every one who aspires to search for his ancestors and to learn his family history. — *Athenæum.*

This is the best compendious genealogist's guide that has yet been published, and Mr. Phillimore deserves the thanks and appreciation of all lovers of family history. — *Reliquary.*

Notice. —Large Paper Edition. A few copies, on hand-made paper, wide margins, bound in half morocco, may be obtained, price $6.50 *net.*

THE KINSHIP OF MEN : An Argument from Pedigrees; or, Genealogy Viewed as a Science. By HENRY KENDALL. Cr. 8vo.   Cloth, $2.00.

The old pedigree-hunting was a sign of pride and pretension; the modern is simply dictated by the desire to know whatever can be known. The one advanced itself by the methods of immoral advocacy; the other proceeds by those of scientific research. — *Spectator* (London).

RECORDS AND RECORD SEARCHING. A Guide to the Genealogist and Topographer. By WALTER RYE. 8vo, cloth.   Price $2.50.

This book places in the hands of the Antiquary and Genealogist, and others interested in kindred studies, a comprehensive guide to the enormous mass of material which is available in his researches, showing what it consists of, and where it can be found.

ANCESTRAL TABLETS. A Collections of Diagrams for Pedigrees, so arranged that Eight Generations of the Ancestors of any Person may be recorded in a connected and simple form. By WILLIAM H. WHITMORE, A. M.   SEVENTH EDITION. *On heavy parchment paper, large 4to, tastefully and strongly bound, Roxburgh style.* Price $2.00.

" No one with the least bent for genealogical research ever examined this ingeniously compact substitute for the 'family tree' without longing to own it. It provides for the recording of eight lineal generations, and is a perpetual incentive to the pursuit of one's ancestry." — *Nation.*

THE ELEMENTS OF HERALDRY. A practical manual, showing what heraldry is, where it comes from, and to what extent it is applicable to American usage; to which is added a Glossary in English, French and Latin of the forms employed.   Profusely Illustrated.   By W. H. WHITMORE, author of " Ancestral Tablets," etc.   [*In press.*

Cupples and Hurd,   *Publishers, Booksellers, Library Agents,*   *BOSTON.*

Important New Books.

RECENT FICTION.

Admirable in Quality.   Thoroughly Interesting.   Specially
adapted for Public Libraries and Private Reading.

Each volume substantially bound in Cloth.

*For sale by all Booksellers, or mailed, postpaid, to any address on
receipt of price.*

CUPPLES & HURD, PUBLISHERS, 94 Boylston St., Boston.